33017017023099

Immigration

by Richard Brownell

LUCENT BOOKS
A part of Gale, Cengage Learning

GALE
CENGAGE Learning

Detroit • New York • San Francisco • New Haven, Conn • Waterville, Maine • London

This book is dedicated to Zoltan, who is my greatest source of support.

LIBRARY OF CONGRESS CATALOGING-IN-PUBLICATION DATA

Brownell, Richard.
  Immigration / by Richard Brownell.
    p. cm. – (Hot topics)
  Includes bibliographical references and index.
  ISBN 978-1-59018-993-1 (hardcover : alk. paper)
  1. United States–Emigration and immigration. 2. Illegal aliens--United States. I. Title.
  JV6465.B72 2008
  304.8'73–dc22

                                                    2007036700

ISBN-10: 1-59018-993-0

Printed in the United States of America
 2 3 4 5 6 7 12 11 10 09 08

CONTENTS

FOREWORD   **4**

INTRODUCTION   **6**
The Debate Over Immigration

CHAPTER ONE   **11**
The History of Immigration in America

CHAPTER TWO   **26**
The New Face of Immigration

CHAPTER THREE   **42**
 The Economics of Immigration

CHAPTER FOUR   **62**
Assimilation and Identity

CHAPTER FIVE   **77**
Calls for Reform

NOTES   **96**

DISCUSSION QUESTIONS   **101**

ORGANIZATIONS TO CONTACT   **103**

FOR MORE INFORMATION   **105**

INDEX   **108**

PICTURE CREDITS   **112**

ABOUT THE AUTHOR   **112**

FOREWORD

Young people today are bombarded with information. Aside from traditional sources such as newspapers, television, and the radio, they are inundated with a nearly continuous stream of data from electronic media. They send and receive e-mails and instant messages, read and write online "blogs," participate in chat rooms and forums, and surf the Web for hours. This trend is likely to continue. As Patricia Senn Breivik, former dean of university libraries at Wayne State University in Detroit, states, "Information overload will only increase in the future. By 2020, for example, the available body of information is expected to double every 73 days! How will these students find the information they need in this coming tidal wave of information?"

Ironically, this overabundance of information can actually impede efforts to understand complex issues. Whether the topic is abortion, the death penalty, gay rights, or obesity, the deluge of fact and opinion that floods the print and electronic media is overwhelming. The news media report the results of polls and studies that contradict one another. Cable news shows, talk radio programs, and newspaper editorials promote narrow viewpoints and omit facts that challenge their own political biases. The World Wide Web is an electronic minefield where legitimate scholars compete with the postings of ordinary citizens who may or may not be well-informed or capable of reasoned argument. At times, strongly worded testimonials and opinion pieces both in print and electronic media are presented as factual accounts.

Conflicting quotes and statistics can confuse even the most diligent researchers. A good example of this is the question of whether or not the death penalty deters crime. For instance, one study found that murders decreased by nearly one-third when the death penalty was reinstated in New York in 1995. Death penalty supporters cite this finding to support their argument that the existence of the death penalty deters criminals from committing murder. However, another study found that states without the death penalty have murder rates below the national average. This study is cited by opponents of capital punishment, who reject the claim that the death penalty deters murder. Students need context and clear, informed discussion if they are to think critically and make informed decisions.

The Hot Topics series is designed to help young people wade through the glut of fact, opinion, and rhetoric so that they can think critically about controversial issues. Only by reading and thinking critically will they be able to formulate a viewpoint that is not simply the parroted views of others. Each volume of the series focuses on today's most pressing social issues and provides a balanced overview of the topic. Carefully crafted narrative, fully documented primary and secondary source quotes, informative sidebars, and study questions all provide excellent starting points for research and discussion. Full-color photographs and charts enhance all volumes in the series. With its many useful features, the Hot Topics series is a valuable resource for young people struggling to understand the pressing issues of the modern era.

INTRODUCTION

THE DEBATE OVER IMMIGRATION

May 1, 2007 was a day of protest for tens of thousands of immigrants and the citizens who supported them in the United States. In cities across the country, in groups large and small, people marched, carried signs, sang protest songs, and spoke with television and newspaper reporters eager to hear their stories. They spoke of a desire to become American citizens, to be afforded equal rights under the law, and to claim their share of the American Dream. They have been compared to the millions of immigrants who have come to this country throughout American history, hoping to find a better life than the one they left behind in foreign lands, but they are different in many ways than those who came before them.

A large portion of the immigrants who protested in 2007 were of Hispanic origin, and there has never been a wave of immigration as large as the one the United States is currently experiencing. Among the more than 25 million Hispanic immigrants there are anywhere from 12 to 20 million who are in the United States illegally, meaning they crossed the southern border unauthorized or chose to stay after their temporary visas expired. Their presence in this country has changed the way America thinks about and deals with immigration, and the resulting debate over how to handle immigration has become one of the most hotly debated topics of our time. The large number of foreign-born persons in the United States today impacts how the nation conducts business, how it governs the population, and how Americans see themselves as a people and as a society.

Who Marched and Why

Many of the marchers were workers in low-skill jobs who have lived in the United States for years, but fear deportation because they are illegal immigrants. "After working 22 years here, paying taxes and being a good citizen, I think it's fair they give me residency," said Los Angeles protester Manuel Hernandez, an illegal immigrant from Mexican who marched with his wife and two children. "It's not fair we don't have documents."[1]

Hernandez's story was one that was repeated by many of the 20,000 protestors in Los Angeles that day. In Chicago, 150,000

On May 1, 2007, rallies and protests were held in cities across the United States in support of immigrants' rights.

Many Americans believe that illegal immigrants should not be afforded the same rights as legal U.S. citizens.

took to the streets to protest the breakup of mixed status families, or families in the United States made up of legal and illegal immigrants that could be split up if federal immigration authorities arrest and deport mothers or fathers who cannot prove their documented residency status. A gathering of 5,000 in New York City called for an end to immigration raids that have rounded up thousands of illegal immigrants, as did another of 450 in Washington, DC.

The nationwide event was carried out peacefully, with the exception of a scuffle between police in Los Angeles and a small group of unruly protestors who threw bottles and rocks. Organizers and participants wanted to demonstrate that undocumented workers are hard-working law-abiding people worthy of citizenship, but several counter-demonstrators voiced opposition to granting citizenship to millions of illegal immigrants.

Jerry Hearty of Coolidge, Arizona, was one counter-demonstrator who lost his union-wage job in a meat packing plant in Nebraska many years ago when the company started hiring immigrants at lower wages. "Now, no American can work at a packinghouse anymore because it's all minimum wage, and it's all illegal aliens."[2] Others like Hearty believe that all immigrants should follow the well-established legal process of becoming citizens and that they do not deserve special treatment.

Many were also angered by the fact that the protests took place on May 1, also known as May Day, a labor holiday in communist countries. To them, the date was no coincidence because they believed that illegal immigrants were not interested in becoming Americans, but only in coming to America to take advantage of its resources and its generosity.

What Is at Stake

The protests of May 2007 gave voice to many views about immigration in the United States today and to theories about what should be done with the large and growing illegal population. The event preceded debate over a major immigration reform bill being considered by federal lawmakers in Washington, DC. Among the issues under consideration were creating a path to citizenship for illegal immigrants, tougher border security, stricter enforcement of existing immigration laws, and providing a steady supply of low-skilled workers that American businesses have come to depend on in recent years.

Protestors wanted to have their opinions heard by elected officials, and they refused to be sidelined while their future was decided. It was unclear if the protests had the effect illegal immigrants and their citizen supporters desired. A similar protest on May 1, 2006, which was much larger with one million demonstrators nationwide, led to a backlash against illegal immigration. In the year following that event, several states passed strict laws against hiring illegal immigrants and prohibited them from accessing government services like health care and social welfare. A federal push for stricter enforcement led to the deportation of 195,024 illegal immigrants in 2006, up 21,661 from the previous year. In the first half of 2007, over 125,000 more had been deported, indicating that the trend was increasing substantially.

This backlash was a major reason for the large drop off in participation in the 2007 demonstrations. Many illegal immigrants feared being identified among the marchers and chose to stay away rather than risk being arrested. Whether their actions helped or hurt their cause remains to be seen because the debate still rages. At issue is the future of immigration in this country. America has always been seen as a land of opportunity for people in foreign lands looking to improve their lives. If it is to maintain its unique status as a nation of immigrants, the United States will need to reconcile the conflict that exists between support for immigration and the desire to preserve American identity.

THE HISTORY OF IMMIGRATION IN AMERICA

America is unique in the world in that it has had the most sustained open immigration policy of any nation in modern history. It has accepted more legal immigrants as residents than all the rest of the world combined. Since the establishment of its constitutional government in 1789, America's shores have been the destination for tens of millions of people who left the oppression and poverty of their native lands and risked death on dangerous land and ocean voyages. They came because the United States was a country like no other. It was governed by a democratically elected legislature, which was a novelty in the eighteenth and nineteenth centuries. It also operated on a free market economy that allowed virtually any man to go into business for himself. The only limit to a person's success in America was how hard they were willing to work. The romantic notion was that the United States welcomed people from all nations, no matter their religion, occupation, wealth or poverty, to come into its welcoming arms and eventually become full citizens. The reality was far more complex.

Immigration to the United States was not an easy task for many who completed the voyage across thousands of miles of ocean from Europe and Asia, or crossed the barren desert region separating the United States from Central and South America. People often left behind family and friends in their native countries, in some cases never seeing them again. They often came to this country with little or no knowledge of the English language or American customs, and they had no idea where they would live or how they would earn money. In many cases, they were welcomed by groups dedicated to providing charity to immigrants until they could establish themselves. However, in many other cases they were taken advantage of, and their innocence was exploited by thieves and scam artists.

Despite these hardships, immigrants continued to arrive in America throughout the nineteenth and twentieth centuries in large numbers. The prejudice and hostility that they sometimes experienced at the hands of native-born Americans did not deter them. Even periods of reduced immigration mandated by the federal government never irreversibly stemmed the tide of

The Evolution of the U.S. Census

Since the first census was conducted in 1790, the decennial survey of America and its population adapted to the growing and evolving nation. As noted by the U.S. Census Bureau in a May 2000 pamphlet, *Factfinder for the Nation,*

> Down through the years, the nation's needs and interests became more complex. This meant that there had to be statistics to help people understand what was happening and have a basis for planning. The content of the decennial census changed accordingly. For example, the first inquiry on manufactures was made in 1810.... Questions on agriculture, mining, and fisheries were added in 1840; and in 1850, the census included inquiries on social issues—taxation, churches, pauperism, and crime.

The census also spread geographically, to new states and territories added to the Union a well as to other areas under U.S. sovereignty or jurisdiction.

There were so many more inquiries of all kinds in the censuses of 1880 and 1890 that almost a full decade was needed to publish all the results.... Accordingly, Congress limited the 1900 Census to questions on population, manufactures, agriculture, and mortality. Many of the dropped topics reappeared in later censuses as advances in technology made it possible to process and publish the data faster.

U.S. Census Bureau, *Factfinder for the Nation,* May 2000; http://www.census.gov

newcomers to the United States. As long as America remained a land of opportunity, people from all over the world would continue to look upon it as a destination of hope.

Western European Immigration

The small amount of immigration to the United States in the early years of the American republic was not well documented, and the best population estimates combined with passenger manifests of ships arriving in American ports place the yearly average at 6,000 people up until 1820. The U.S. Census was first conducted in 1790, but it only counted the number of free men and women and slaves. It did not inquire about a person's nation of origin, and it was quite simplistic compared to the modern decennial census.

Turmoil in Europe as a result of the French Revolution of 1789 and the Napoleonic Wars that devastated Europe until 1814 significantly limited immigration. Many able bodied men were drafted into armies of the various warring nations and Europe's war-ravaged economy left little money for private citizens to buy passage on a ship. A number of private shipping companies were pressed into military service or went out of business,

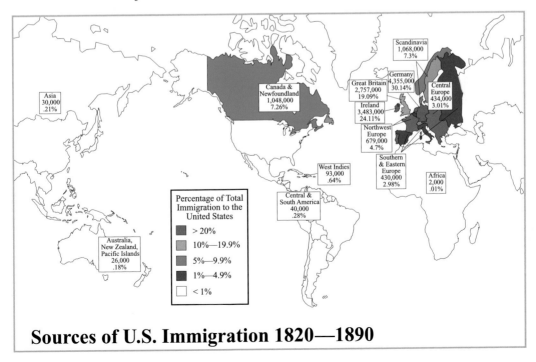

Sources of U.S. Immigration 1820—1890

so there was considerably less trans-Atlantic travel. The war of 1812 between the United States and Great Britain also curtailed immigration because there is little motivation to immigrate to a nation that is at war.

After this period of upheaval, a sustained period of prosperity in the United States led to enormous economic and territorial expansion, two factors that proved very inviting to would-be immigrants. Over 2.5 million immigrants came to America in a thirty-year period beginning in 1820, playing an important role in the rapid growth of the United States population, which rose from 9.6 million that year to just over 23 million in 1850, one of the highest growth rates in the world at that time.

A vast majority of these immigrants came from Western Europe, with the bulk of them from Germany, Ireland, France, and Great Britain. The Irish were driven to America by widespread famine, while the balance of the European arrivals were motivated by economic factors. Europe was rapidly industrializing during this time, and a large numbers of agricultural jobs disappeared as land and labor was lost to factories and commercial expansion. While the United States was also industrializing at

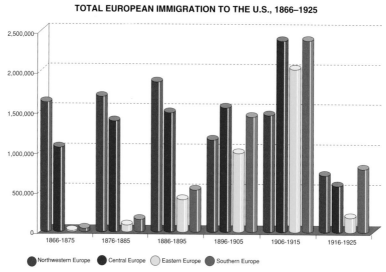

TOTAL EUROPEAN IMMIGRATION TO THE U.S., 1866–1925

Northwestern Europe   Central Europe   Eastern Europe   Southern Europe

Source: Historical Statistics of the United States, Series C-89-119.

A replica of the Irish ship Jeanie Johnston, *which carried hundreds of Irish emigrants to North America during the potato famine from 1848–1855.*

an accelerated rate, there was far more land available for agricultural development. Additionally, the development of steamships and railroads further facilitated the ease of travel across Europe to the coast where passage could be obtained to cross the Atlantic to America.

According to Herbert S. Klein, author of A Population History of the United States, "The post-1830 transoceanic migration to the United States would turn out to be the largest such oceanic migration in world history."[3]

"No Irish Need Apply"

Although it may be an urban myth that this sentiment appeared on virtually every "help wanted" sign, some nineteenth-century newspaper ads for female domestics did indeed include the words, "no Irish need apply." Richard Jensen of the University of Chicago argues that "Evidence from the job market shows no significant discrimination against the Irish—on the contrary, employers eagerly sought them out."

However, the reason for their popularity may have been their willingness to work for low wages at hazardous tasks. According to the Library of Congress,

"The Irish often suffered blatant or subtle job discrimination. Irish immigrants often entered the workforce at the bottom of the occupational ladder and took on the menial and dangerous jobs that were often avoided by other workers…many Irish men labored in coal mines and built railroads and canals. Railroad construction was so dangerous that it was said, '[there was] an Irishman buried under every tie.' As Irish immigrants moved inland from eastern cities, they found themselves in heated competition for jobs. This competition heightened class tensions and, at the turn of the century, Irish Americans were often antagonized by organizations such as the American Protective Association (APA) and the Ku Klux Klan."

University of Illinois, Chicago, http://tigger.uic.edu/~rjensen/no-irish.htm; U.S. Library of Congress, http://memory.loc.gov/learn/features/immig/irish4.html

From 1850, the American population began to feel the effects of large-scale immigration. Until 1830, immigrants accounted for only 1.5 percent of the population. By 1850, when the U.S. Census began recording place of birth, immigrants had risen to 10 percent of the population. The California Gold Rush of 1849 brought the first significant wave of immigration from nations outside Europe, with immigrants arriving from China, Australia, Mexico, and South America. Additionally, the end of the Mexican War in 1848 resulted in the United States gaining a large amount of territory from Mexico, leading to the automatic U.S. citizenship of 80,000 to 100,000 Mexicans living in that region.

Europeans continued to dominate immigration during this period despite the addition of these other nationalities. Between 1850 and 1930, five million Germans immigrated to the United States, along with 3.5 million British and 4.5 million Irish. The onset of the American Civil War in 1861 slowed immigration, and the foreign-born population of the United States grew by only a little more than one million during this period, but after 1870, it picked up again. After this point, a new wave of immigrants began coming to the United States

Southern and Eastern European Immigrants

While immigrants would continue to arrive in a steady stream from Western Europe, the number who arrived from Southern and Eastern Europe began to rise sharply in the last decades of the nineteenth century. The industrialization and resultant economic prosperity in Western Europe did not spread to the south and east, and immigrants from those areas fled the poor economic and social conditions with growing frequency. In 1870, the census reported 93,824 foreign-born persons from Eastern and Southern Europe, which accounted for 6 percent of all immigrants. By 1910, over 4.5 million foreign-born persons from Eastern and Southern Europe were living in the U.S, coming mainly from Poland, Russia, and Italy. By this point, nearly two-thirds of all immigrants came from Eastern and Southern Europe.

With the arrival of people from this region, the general makeup of European immigration began to change, and with it

Many immigrants arriving in the United States found themselves living in rundown, crowded conditions, such as this depiction of a New York City neighborhood in the late 1800s.

America's attitude toward immigrants. Most of the immigrants from Western Europe were light skinned and generally of the Protestant religion, which was the predominant religious faith of the United States. The Irish, who were Catholic, were a notable exception, and they faced numerous difficulties in the United States because of their Catholic faith. Groups of Protestant Americans like the Order of the Star-Spangled Banner and the Order of United Americans heaped scorn and ridicule, and sometimes violence, upon Catholics from Ireland and other nations mainly because they feared that the continued arrival of Catholic immigrants would threaten their majority in the United States. Irish Catholics in particular were often turned away from employers and ended up taking up public sector jobs in many cities as police officers and other municipal workers.

Many of the immigrants from Eastern and Southern Europe also faced racism because they were dark-skinned, which made them visibly different from the majority of the population. Jewish immigrants often remained within their own communities and rarely mixed with outsiders, which made many native-born Americans suspicious of them. Their religion was also looked upon as strange by many citizens in a nation that was overwhelmingly Christian.

The Jews, Irish, and other poor immigrants from Europe often settled in urban areas that were predominantly poor and filthy. The conditions of these neighborhoods was a result of poor urban planning and a complete lack of municipal services like trash collection, sewage treatment, and health codes; all things taken for granted today. However, during this period of high immigration, the immigrants themselves were blamed for the squalid conditions of the inner cities.

Francis Walker captured the scorn many native-born Americans felt in the *Atlantic Monthly* in 1896.

> For nearly two generations, great numbers of persons utterly unable to earn their living, by reason of one or another form of physical or mental disability, and others who were, from widely different causes, unfit to be members of any decent community, were admitted to our ports without challenge or question.

> The question to-day is, not of preventing the wards of our almshouses, our insane asylums, and our jails from being stuffed to repletion by new arrivals from Europe; but of protecting the American rate of wages, the American standard of living, and the quality of American citizenship from degradation through the tumultuous access of

vast throngs of ignorant and brutalized peasantry from the countries of eastern and southern Europe.[4]

Long before Walker's words gave voice to the scorn many felt over the immigrants of Eastern and Southern Europe, the federal government began taking strict control of immigration.

Closing the Door to Immigrants

Immigration policy was left mainly to the states for the first seventy years of American history, but a series of Supreme Court decisions in 1849 known as the Passenger Cases began chipping away at state control. The federal government had grown irate at the collection of special taxes from immigrants by several states, and the court ruled that they did not have the power to collect such taxes. Congress went further in 1864, passing legislation that took control of immigration policy from the states, and by

A group of immigrants files across the dock at Ellis Island, the national reception center for people seeking entry into the United States.

1875, the Supreme Court had effectively ruled that the establishment and regulation of immigration policy fell under the federal government's constitutional power to regulate interstate commerce. This was done in part to bring order to a chaotic system in which scattered state procedures over immigration often contradicted one another.

Once these Supreme Court precedents were established, the federal government stepped in to create a structured system to control immigration. The first federal act to deliberately set a standard was the Chinese Exclusion Act of 1882. This act rose out of complaints about the 290,000 Chinese immigrants who had settled in the Western U.S. since the California Gold Rush, seeking to escape turbulent political conditions in China. Many found work as cheap labor on the railroads and as domestic servants in California and the western territories, where they were blamed for driving down wages. The Exclusion Act's passage barred Chinese immigration to the United States for a period of ten years and was renewed several times until it was repealed in 1943.

In 1892, when the 9.2 million immigrants in the United States represented 15 percent of the population, the federal government took control of immigration at the Port of New York, establishing Ellis Island as the national reception center for people seeking entry into the United States. Everyone who came to Ellis Island and other ports of entry were subjected to literacy tests and health examinations. Those with tuberculosis or other communicable diseases were either turned back or forced to live in quarantine for extended periods of time. The literacy tests were an attempt to control the quality of immigrants who were let into the country. People were further evaluated for the labor skills they possessed, which allowed the government to keep an overabundance of workers with particular job skills from driving down wages for citizens.

In 1907, Senator William P. Dillingham established the United States Immigration Commission. This body, historically known as the Dillingham Commission, investigated the occupations and living standards of immigrants in the United States, and came to the biased conclusion that immigrants from Eastern

and Southern Europe possessed a higher risk for criminal behavior, poverty, illness, and lower intelligence than immigrants
who had come to America previously.

LIBERTY THROUGH IMMIGRATION

"Liberty depends on a society that allows people the freedom to
migrate and live where they can best build a life for themselves.
A society that has to compete to attract new and productive citizens will be compelled by necessity to fight for the freedom of its
members—even for those who were afforded fewer legal rights
because of the circumstances of their birth."

Brendan Miniter, "Let Their People Come," *Wall Street Journal*, July 3, 2003.

Based in part on the results of the Dillingham Commission, the federal government passed a series of strict immigration quotas to limit the number of people coming from foreign
shores. The Emergency Quota Act of 1921 limited the number
of immigrants from each nation to three percent of that nation's
total population in the United States as reported in the 1910
Census. This act heavily favored immigration from Western
Europe because immigrants had been coming from this region
for much longer, resulting in higher populations in the United
States. The National Origins Act of 1924 further restricted immigration from each country to two percent of that nation's total
population in the United States in 1890. Together, these acts effectively ended mass immigration in the United States for much
of the rest of the twentieth century.

Immigration in the Twentieth Century

In 1921, the year the first quota act was passed, 800,000 immigrants came to the United States. By the late 1920s, that number
fell to 300,000. The installation of the National Origins Act in
1929 capped immigration at a total of 150,000 per year, but
the Great Depression did more to slow the influx of foreigners
than any federal law. With a third of the nation out of work for
much of the 1930s, there were no jobs to draw immigrants, and
overall immigration slowed to a comparative trickle, with a low

point of only 23,000 entering the country in 1933.

World War II continued to keep immigration low, but the federal government did allow several thousand Mexican laborers into the country to work in agricultural jobs. Known as the Bracero Program, this use of temporary labor offset the large number of jobs left open by the drafting of millions of able-bodied male citizens into the armed forces. By 1945, 50,000 Mexican workers were filling American agricultural jobs, and another 75,000 were working in the railroad industry.

After the allied victory brought an end to World War II in 1945, the American economy grew tremendously, but immigration was still controlled by strict quotas. The McCarren-Walter Immigration Act of 1952 reaffirmed the national-origins quota system, capping immigration at 175,000 per year. Various refugee relief acts did allow 600,000 individuals from war-torn countries in Europe and Asia into the United States in the late 1940s and early 1950s. Additionally, the War Brides Acts of 1945 and 1946 allowed foreign-born wives and fiancés of U.S. servicemen to immigrate.

In 1954, the federal government carried out a mass deportation of thousands of illegal immigrants from Mexico. It was estimated in the de-

A group of bracero workers crosses the border from Mexico into Hidalgo, Texas.

President Lyndon B. Johnson, seated, signed the Immigration and Nationality Act in 1965, which removed many of the immigration quotas that had been in place for years.

cade preceding this deportation the number of illegal immigrants had risen 6000 percent, with one million coming in 1954 alone, taking advantage of the open border and high number of available jobs. The U.S. Border Patrol, with the help of federal, state, and local authorities in Texas, Arizona, New Mexico, and California succeeded in driving many back into Mexico voluntarily. It was unknown exactly how many returned to their native country of their own choice, or if they remained in Mexico or simply crossed back into the United States after the sweep ended.

The Immigration and Nationality Act of 1965 and After

In 1965, the U.S. Congress passed the Immigration and Nationality Act which effectively removed many of the immigration quotas that had been in place for decades. An annual limit of 170,000 visas was established for immigrants from countries in the Eastern Hemisphere with no more than 20,000 per country. Another cap of 120,000 immigrants from the Western Hemisphere was also put in place, with visas available on a first-come, first-serve basis. There was no cap placed on family reunification visas, which created a chain migration that allowed immigrants who attained citizenship to sponsor the immigration of adult relatives.

THE IMPACT OF IMMIGRATION

"The impact of immigration—legal and illegal—on jobs, schools, health care, the environment, national security, are all very serious problems. But more serious than all of them put together is this threat to the culture. I believe we are in a clash of civilizations."

Representative Tom Tancredo (R-CO), quoted in Kirk Johnson, "Anxiety in the Land of the Anti-Immigration Crusader," *New York Times,* June 24, 2007.

After the passage of the Immigration and Nationality Act, immigration was once again on the rise. In the 1970s, 4.5 million people came to the United States, with Latin Americans comprising 44 percent of the total. Another 7.3 million immigrants entered the country in the 1980s, and 10 million more came in the 1990s. Along with these legal immigrants came wave after wave of illegal immigrants, with approximately 500,000 per year entering the United States during the 1990s. In the first years of the twenty-first century, legal immigration to the United States averaged about one million people per year, but illegal immigration averaged an additional 700,000 per year during the same period.

The largest group of immigrants in this post-1965 wave were from Latin America, and their percentage of the foreign-born population rises every year. Although immigrants still come to the United States from Europe, their numbers are but a fraction of what they once were. They lost their majority status among foreign-born people in the United States in the 1980 census, signifying the end of an era of American immigration. As a new era of Latin American immigration begins, the United States can no longer look to the past to predict what effect the immigrants of the twenty-first century will have. As a nation of immigrants, America is heading into uncharted territory.

THE NEW FACE OF IMMIGRATION

America has always been a draw for people from other nations looking for a better life with greater economic and social opportunities. While immigration to the United States has been virtually continuous since its founding, a review of historical trends demonstrates that the number of immigrants entering the United States rose and fell largely in response to economic and legislative factors. In times of economic prosperity, America has been a beacon for foreigners searching for better jobs who have been welcomed by a vast commercial and industrial base that thrived on fresh sources of labor. The American economy, measured in terms of gross domestic product (GDP), which is the total value of all goods and services produced within the nation's borders, was $11.7 trillion in 2006, the largest in the world, and with growth estimated at 3.3 percent annually. This economic dynamism, combined with the country's open door policy, which has set virtually no quotas or restrictions on immigration since 1965, has set the stage for the largest immigration wave the United States has ever experienced.

"The percentage of the population that was born abroad is slightly lower than it was when the last great wave of immigrants arrived, at the beginning of the twentieth century: 11 percent now compared to 15 percent then," notes Tamara Jacoby, editor of *Reinventing the Melting Pot: the New Immigrants and What it Means to be American* and senior fellow at the Manhattan Institute, an organization dedicated to urban policy research. She goes on to add, however, "the absolute number of newcomers living in the United States today is the highest it has ever been."[5] The Census Bureau places that number at 40 million, with 53

How the U.S. Census Counts Americans

The United States government has conducted a nationwide census to determine the size of the American population every ten years since 1790. The valuable statistical information collected by the census aids in the drawing of congressional districts and the distribution of federal and state money for social services, currently totaling $200 billion annually. Recent changes in the how the census is conducted reflect the rapid growth of communities and ethnic groups in the United States, and the greater reliance by the governments, community organizations, and businesses on the data that is gathered.

From the U.S. Census Web site:

In the past, most households received a short-form questionnaire, while one household in six received a long form that contained additional questions and provided more detailed socioeconomic information about the population.

The 2010 Census will be a short-form only census and will count all residents living in the United States as well as ask for name, sex, age, date of birth, race, ethnicity, relationship and housing tenure…

The more detailed socioeconomic information is now collected through the American Community Survey. The survey provides current data about your community every year, rather than once every 10 years. It is sent to a small percentage of the population on a rotating basis throughout the decade. No household will receive the survey more often than once every five years.

U.S. Census Bureau Web site, http://www.census.gov/2010census/about_2010_census/007622.html

percent originating from Latin America, 25 percent from Asia, and the remaining 22 percent from other regions.

This wave is unique not only because it is the largest in absolute numbers, but also because it is predominantly Latin American in character. No other immigration wave in American history has been so heavily skewed toward one ethnic group. The implications this Latin American wave will have on the nation are far reaching and have the potential to change how Americans view immigration and how they perceive their country as a whole.

The Latin American Immigrant Wave

Hispanics are the fastest growing ethnic group in the United States, recently surpassing African Americans as the largest minority with 44 million, or 14 percent of the total population. Immigration from Latin America has certainly aided in this growth; 28 percent of Hispanics in this country are foreign-born. Additionally, one in three Hispanic immigrants are from Mexico, and Mexicans account for approximately 67 percent of all Hispanics, both foreign- and native-born, in the United States, making them the largest national group within the Hispanic community. As with other immigrants from Central and South America, Mexicans come to the United States mainly for economic reasons.

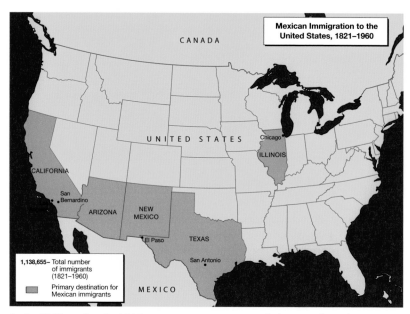

In the 1800s and early 1900s Mexican immigrants settled primarily in the southwest United States. Today, Mexican populations are found across the United States.

Mexico is a poor nation when compared to its northern neighbor, with a GDP of $676.5 billion that is only a fraction of America's $11.7 trillion. The GDP per person in Mexico was only $6,450 per person in 2006, while the U.S. GDP per person averaged $39,000. Jobs in Mexico are scarce and pay little, while jobs in the United States are plentiful, particularly in the farming, construction, and service industries. These low-skill occupations pay little compared to other jobs in the United States, but the salaries are frequently many times higher than similar work would pay in Mexico. For instance, dairy work-

Spanish Language Television

The first Spanish-language television station in the United States went on the air in San Antonio, Texas, in 1961. Since that time, Hispanic television entertainment has grown into a multi-billion-dollar business, and Univision is leading the way as America's largest Spanish-language network:

- The Univision Network is by far the nation's most watched Spanish-language broadcast television network and the fifth most-watched full-time network overall, competing head-to-head with the English-language television networks in primetime seven nights a week.
- Since Nielsen Media introduced its Hispanic Television Index in 1992, the Univision Network has led all other networks (Spanish or English-language, cable or broadcast) in sustained viewer growth.
- As the first and foremost Spanish-language broadcast television network in the United States, the Univision Network attracts more Hispanics during each broadcast hour than any other network (English- or Spanish-language).
- More Hispanics watch the Univision Network in each [programming segment] than ABC, CBS, NBC, FOX and Telemundo.
- Hispanic viewing share levels have increased from 59% in 1992 to 78% in 2003.
- Univision consistently airs on average all of the top 20 programs on Spanish-language television.

Univision Web site, http://www.univision.net/corp/en/univision.jsp

ers in Mexico earn approximately $8 to $12 per day, while a survey conducted by the Cornell University Cooperative Extension of Hispanic dairy workers in New York State determined that wages averaged $7.50 per hour. Factory workers do not fair much better. Unionized autoworkers in the United States earn at least $27 per hour plus benefits, while experienced autoworkers in Mexico earn approximately $3.50 per hour. This disparity has led many in Mexico to move to the United States with the hope of finding better jobs.

Mexicans, as well as people from poor Latin American countries such as Guatemala and Honduras, travel to wherever jobs can be found within the United States, but they have traditionally migrated to major metropolitan areas in four states—California, New York, Texas, and Florida—which are home to 26 million immigrants. Within these areas, large Hispanic communities, or enclaves, have been established which resemble their native lands where business and politics is conducted in Spanish and Hispanic cultural traditions are prominent in everyday life.

The Impact on American Cities

The growth of Hispanic communities in the United States has led to a debate about the impact of mass immigration on America's urban centers. City dwellers across the U.S. consume vast amounts of water, food, electricity, and other items that must be carefully measured by urban planners to prevent shortages. Through the study of birth rates and the migration trends of the native-born population, planners can predict increasing and decreasing demand for a variety of systems necessary to successful urban management like water and sewage treatment, power supply, and transportation. However, it is difficult to meet the needs of cities with large immigrant communities because they grow faster than urban planners can account for and adapt to their needs.

The Federation for American Immigration Reform (FAIR), a national lobbying group that seeks improved border security and stricter controls on immigration, claims that these communities, which grow larger every year, are primarily responsible for urban sprawl, which is the unrestricted outward growth of cities that often harms the surrounding environment and puts a strain on natural resources. "For the sake of the environment, we must oppose immigration-driven population growth. Stopping America's rapid population growth is necessary for the sake of the environment and for the preservation of life for future generations."[6]

ENFORCING THE LAW

"The fact is that most illegals are coming here to work. Take away the jobs and they'll return home. Again, lawmakers have already passed the necessary laws. They simply need to make sure those laws ... are fully enforced."

Rich Tucker, *Townhall.com,* June 15, 2007.

Demographer William Frey of the Brookings Institution, an independent research group, points out, "A lot of cities rely on immigration to prop up their housing market and prop up their economies."[7] He suggests that if it were not for the influx of immigrants, many of these cities would be experiencing shrinking populations as native Americans move to suburban or rural areas. For instance, without the one million immigrants who came to New York City from 2000 to 2006, the area would have lost nearly 600,000 people.

While there are differing views of the impact of immigration on American cities, the level of Mexican migration to the United States in particular has reached record proportions. Since 2000, migration to the United States has been a larger drain on the Mexican population than death. "Mexico's demographics agency found that an average of 577,000 people migrated to the U.S. each year between 2000-2005," according to the Associated Press, "compared to 495,000 deaths a year in the same period."[8] Put another way, 10 percent of all born Mexicans are currently living in the United States. However, not all Mexican immigrants have come into the United States legally. In fact, it is estimated that 78 percent of all Mexicans who traveled to the United States from 2001 to 2005 came illegally, a statistic that has caused significant alarm among U.S. lawmakers and citizens.

Counting the Illegal Immigrants

Illegal immigrants tend to fall into one of two categories: those who cross the border unauthorized and those who were admitted legally and have overstayed their visas. They are motivated to come to the United States for economic reasons much like legal immigrants, however, there are additional factors that drive them to cross the U.S.-Mexico border illegally or refuse to leave after their visas have expired. Applying for a work visa or citizenship in the United States is a complicated process that can involve long waits of months or even years. Many who wish to come to the United States to work would rather forego the bureaucracy because their principle desire is to make money, not become U.S. citizens. Most do not intend to stay in America indefinitely, though many end up doing just that, in some cases encouraging family members to join them after they have established themselves, creating what is called a chain migration that adds to the number of illegal immigrants.

HARD WORK DOESN'T EQUAL CITIZENSHIP

"If they come here illegally just to work, they have not earned citizenship. We are all immigrants, but we did not come here illegally and expect to get citizenship."

Senator Christopher Bond (R-MO), quoted in Robert Pear and John Holusha, "Senate Blocks Effort to Revive Immigration Overhaul," *New York Times,* June 28, 2007.

It is difficult to determine how many illegal immigrants there are in the United States, and estimates vary widely. The very nature of their undocumented status makes it difficult to locate and track them, and many do their best to maintain a low profile by not paying taxes and avoiding census surveys. The Census Bureau is not empowered by legislative mandate to ask the citizenship status of respondents, but it does estimate that there are 12 million illegal immigrants in the United States. This

Mexican and other Central American immigrants entering the United States illegally often face grueling and dangerous conditions while crossing the U.S.–Mexico border.

is the number most often quoted in the media, and it is generally accepted by the federal government to be accurate. However, a report issued by Bear Stearns Asset Management Inc., a global investment banking firm, disputes this estimate and places the number of illegal immigrants in the United States at 20 million or more.

Bear Stearns Senior Managing Director Robert Justich and emerging-markets economist Betty Ng, the authors of the report, point out that illegal immigrants avoid taking surveys, in part because they fear being caught and deported. Yet surveys are the principle manner in which the Census Bureau conducts its counts. "The [Current Population Survey], the Census Bureau, the Urban Institute, and the former INS (now part of the

Department of Homeland Security) all use similar processes to determine the total number of immigrants, and which immigrants should be categorized as legal and illegal," wrote Justich and Ng. "In essence, this has created a circular equation that relies on a singular source of inaccurate statistics that gives the impression of independent, multiple verifications."[9]

Justich and Ng focused on state and municipal statistics that they believed provided a more accurate representation of illegal immigration. In studying the total value of remittances, which are transfers of money that foreign workers send to relatives in their native countries, housing permits and school enrollment in predominantly immigrant communities, and factories and towns along the southern U.S. border, the authors concluded that 20 million is a far more accurate number of illegal immigrants currently in the country.

Catching the Illegal Immigrants

Although immigrants can be jailed and deported for being in the United States illegally, criminal enforcement of illegal immigration is a recent phenomenon, arising mainly from concerns that their large number is putting a strain on government resources. Previously, the lack of immigration enforcement and poor security along the 2,000-mile southern border allowed millions of illegal immigrants to come into the United States without fear of being caught. Many of those who were arrested would often disappeared back into the population after being freed pending court hearings. In addition, government agencies in charge of tracking expired visas could not keep track of the backlog that developed with large numbers of immigrants, allowing illegal immigrants to continue living unauthorized in the United States.

In early 2006, Immigration and Customs Enforcement (ICE), the federal agency in charge of tracking down and apprehending illegal immigrants, began conducting raids in cities around

OPPOSITE: *In the 2000s, the U.S. Border Patrol increased its presence along the border with Mexico in an effort to decrease the amount of illegal immigrants crossing into the United States.*

the country where illegal immigrants are widely known to be living and working. The U.S. Border Patrol has also increased its presence along the southern border. Border agent Randy Clark noted in Eagle Pass, Texas, that a year ago, "you could sit here and watch dozens of (illegal immigrants) come out of those houses on the other side of the [Rio Grande] and wade across.... Groups of 40 or 50 or 60 would come across in broad daylight, and just cross in a straight line."[10] Now Clark sees few if any illegal immigrants in this area.

The odds against getting caught are still worth the risk for many who want to make money and take advantages of the opportunities that America has to offer. However, getting caught and returned to their native country is only one danger that illegal immigrants face. Crossing the border can be extremely hazardous, particularly in the summer months when desert temperatures can reach higher than 110 degrees Fahrenheit (43 degrees Centigrade). Every year hundreds of illegal immigrants die or suffer dehydration and heat stroke due to exposure. Dr.

At a section of the Mexico–U.S. border, this sign reads "Danger. Venomous animals" to warn those attempting to illegally cross the desert into the United States of possible dangers they may encounter.

Samuel Keim, an associate professor of emergency medicine at the University of Arizona, created an index to inform illegal immigrants which days were the most dangerous for attempting a border crossing. "These people are dying on U.S. soil. This is a U.S. issue. It's not a Mexico issue," noted Keim. "If 100 people died anywhere in a single county from exposure, I think it would make national news."[11]

WELFARE COSTS

"By the late 1990s immigrant households were fifty percent more likely to receive means-tested aid than native-born households. Moreover, immigrants appear to assimilate into welfare use. The longer immigrants live in the U.S., the more likely they are to use welfare."

Robert Rector, "Amnesty and Continued Low Skill Immigration Will Substantially Raise Welfare Costs and Poverty," *The Heritage Foundation*, May 12, 2006. http://www.heritage.org/Research/Immigration/bg1936.cfm

The Mexican government issued an illustrated manual to apprise border crossers of the dangers posed by the elements, and pro-immigration groups have voluntarily placed water stations along popular desert routes that illegal immigrants travel. Such actions have drawn criticism from groups who believe these actions only encourage illegal immigration. Barbara Coe, founder of the California Coalition for Immigration Reform, a political advocacy group that supports the election of representatives and legislation that reduces immigration, stated, "That's called aiding and abetting. Illegal aliens are criminals. They can save their lives by staying home."[12]

Illegal immigrants are also at the mercy of smugglers, referred to as coyotes by the U.S. Border Patrol. These smugglers often take advantage of immigrants by charging high fees to aid them in crossing the border undetected. They have been known to leave border crossers lost in the desert or sell them into indentured servitude to dishonest business owners in the United States who force illegal immigrants to work and live in terrible conditions. There is little choice for immigrants in these situations because they fear that calling the police will lead to their own deportation.

Poverty and Crime among Immigrants

Getting to America is a great ordeal for many immigrants, but many of those who get here continue to face tough living conditions. According to a report published by the Census Bureau in 2004, 16 percent of all foreign-born persons were living below the poverty level, compared to 11 percent of the native-born population. Among the foreign-born population living in poverty, Hispanics composed the largest group with 21 percent. Additionally, 41 percent of Hispanic immigrants earn less than $20,000 per year, while 83.4 percent of native-born Americans earn more than $20,000. This economic inequality presents a significant challenge to the success of the Hispanic immigrant community in the United States.

The single best cure for poverty is education, because it provides individuals with greater job opportunities that allow them to raise their income level and economic worth. Unfortunately Hispanic immigrants also lag in this area. The 2004 Census report notes that only 41 percent of Hispanic immigrants over age 25 had completed their high school education, compared with 87.5 percent of native-born Americans.

The lack of education and high poverty levels among Hispanic immigrants has generated concern that the immigrant community is a breeding ground for criminal activity. A 2007 report conducted by Family Security Matters, an advocacy group concerned with home and community security matters, states that the 267,000 illegal immigrants currently in jail in the United States are responsible for close to 1.3 million crimes from drug trafficking to rape and murder. Ruben G. Rumbaut, a sociology professor at the University of California, Irvine, disputes the message that these numbers send, noting, "The misperception that immigrants, especially illegal immigrants, are responsible for higher crime rates is deeply rooted in American public opinion and is sustained by media anecdotes and popular myth."[13] Supporting Rumbaut's statement is a study by the Immigration

Some law enforcement officials believe that investigating the immigration status of gang members and deporting those found guilty of crimes is the most effective way of combating the violent crime associated with gangs.

Policy Center, a pro-immigration group in Washington, DC, that concludes that nationwide incarceration rates among young men in every ethnic group are lowest for immigrants.

Crime statistics for Los Angeles County, home to the largest Hispanic immigrant community in the United States, tell a different story. In 2006 the city of Los Angeles experienced a 15.7 percent increase in gang-related crime, and local law enforcement turned to federal agencies for aid in cracking down on gangs. Screenings by federal agents of jailed gang members revealed that 20 percent of L.A. County Jail inmates and 10 percent of nearby Orange County Jail inmates were illegal immigrants. This has prompted calls for police officers to start inquiring about suspects' immigration status; however this conflicts with the Los Angeles Police Department's Special Order 40, which prohibits officers from making such inquiries. Judicial Watch, a legal advocacy group, has filed a lawsuit against the LAPD to repeal the order.

ACHIEVING SUCCESS

"I am 100% sure that the upward mobility of Hispanics will continue," he says. "I've seen it in my work. I've seen it in the data. I've seen it in my own family."

Juan Guillermo Tornoe, advertising executive in Austin who immigrated from Guatemala. Quoted in Dennis Cauchon, "Generation Gap? About $200,000," *USA Today,* May 21, 2007.

"[Police chiefs] have [supported Special Order 40] because they understand that in a city as under-policed as Los Angeles is, we need to focus on crime," noted Los Angeles Mayor Antonio Villaraigosa. "We need to ensure that the victims of crime, the witnesses of crime come forward. We don't want them to believe we're going to report them to ICE when they do come forward and report a crime."[14]

Some law enforcement officials and criminal prosecutors believe that investigating the immigration status of gang members and deporting those found guilty of crimes is the most effective way of combating the violent crime and drug trafficking that is inherent to the proliferation of gangs. "Undocumented immigrants are a large source of the members of gangs and have been part of the surge that has occurred in the San Fernando Valley," says L.A. attorney Rocky Delgadillo. "If we know there are gang members, we should be in the position to discern every law they have broken, including whether they have come here illegally."[15]

The challenges presented by crime, poverty, and lack of education among legal and illegal immigrants have raised concerns among citizens and public officials alike. There are conflicting views as to how best address these issues, as well as a growing anxiety over whether the federal, state, and local governments

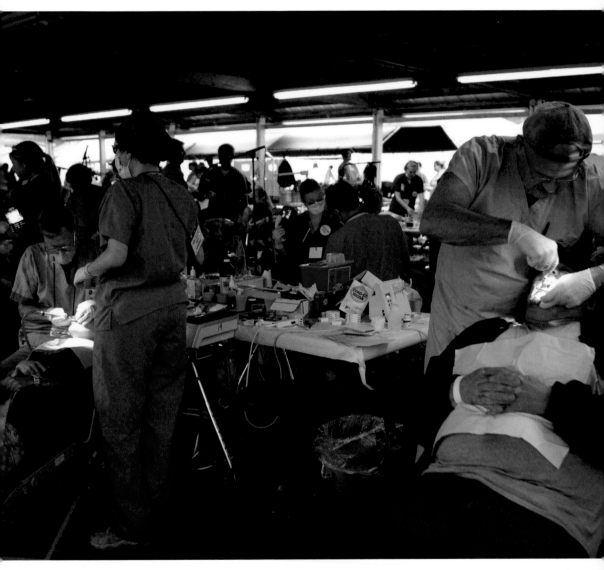

Some hospitals and health care programs treat low-income residents, including illegal immigrants, who otherwise cannot afford health care, for free.

have the resources available to do so while meeting the growing needs of the large immigrant population in the United States.

THE ECONOMICS OF IMMIGRATION

Supporters of open immigration believe the high proportion of immigrant labor in the American work force has had a positive impact on the U.S. economy, contributing to low unemployment and higher profit margins across many industries. Highly skilled immigrants with college educations, many of whom are from Asia, have met the growing demand of technological firms, while low-skill immigrants, predominantly among the Latin American immigrant wave, have bolstered the construction and service industries.

"Immigrants play an important part in the success of America's free-enterprise economy," noted Daniel T. Griswold, Director of Trade Policy Studies for the Cato Institute, a Washington, DC, policy organization that engages in scholarly research and advocacy of various legislative proposals. "They gravitate to occupations where the supply of workers falls short of demand, typically among the higher-skilled and lower-skilled occupations."[16]

Critics of immigration maintain that the benefits do not outweigh the costs imposed on the system by the large number of poor, uneducated, and illegal immigrants. These immigrants take advantage of the same state and federal government services that citizens do, including public school education and medical and social welfare programs, but they pay little or no taxes, thus creating a net drain of government resources. "Although there are economic benefits to cheap, illegal labor, there are significant costs associated with circumventing the labor laws," wrote Robert Justich and Betty Ng in the 2005 Bear Stearns report. "The social expenses of health care, retirement funding, educa-

Are We a Nation of Settlers or a Nation of Immigrants?

America is often referred to as a nation of immigrants, but Samuel Huntington, author of "Who Are We? The Challenge to America's National Identity," disagrees:

> Settlers and immigrants differ fundamentally. Settlers leave an existing society, usually in a group, in order to create a new community... they subscribe to a compact or charter that defines the basis of the community they create... Immigrants, in contrast, do not create a new society. They move from one society to a difference society. Migration is usually a personal process, involving individuals and families, who individually define their relation to their old and new countries. The seventeenth- and eighteenth-century setters came to America because it was a [blank slate]... no society was there; and they came in order to create societies that embodied and would reinforce the culture and values they brought with them from their origin country. Immigrants came later because they wanted to become part of the society the settlers had created.... Before immigrants could come to America, settlers had to found America.

Samuel Huntington, *Who Are We? The Challenges to America's National Identity.* New York, Simon & Schuster, 2004, p. 39-40.

tion and law enforcement are potentially [growing by] $30 billion per year."[17]

It is true that state and federal governments are paying more money to meet the social welfare needs of the growing population, but there is uncertainty as to how much is due to poor and illegal immigrants or whether the income taxes they do pay are actually covering the additional cost. One area that is clearly creating a drain on government resources is the increased cost of securing the southern U.S. border and enforcing immigration laws that are being broken by illegal immigrants and the companies that hire them. Many business owners argue that the latest surge in federal enforcement will harm the economy by taking away the cheap labor that immigrants represent, but many more citizens and government representatives see this as the best way to reduce the growing costs associated with illegal immigration.

A Growing Economic Burden?

The federal and state governments raise the money required to provide public services and benefits to the population by collecting various taxes on income and the manufacture and sale of goods and private services. The poor segment of the population is more reliant on public services than are the middle and upper classes, but poor individuals and families generally pay less in taxes because their income and purchasing power is lower. Critics of immigration have drawn the connection that low-skill immigrants, particularly those in the country illegally, who fall into this category represent a net drain on government resources.

A report published in May 2007 by the Heritage Foundation, a policy organization dedicated to immigration reform, determined that the 4.5 million low-skill legal and illegal immigrant households in the United States, representing 15.9 million people, received $30,160 per household in social welfare and educational services in 2004. These same households paid $10,573 in taxes that same year, which led to a fiscal deficit of $19,587 that had to be picked up by other portions of the population. The implications are that these immigrants are putting a severe strain on public services like schools and hospitals.

Supporters of immigration believe this is an unfair characterization of immigrants, since native poor people in the United States also represent a net drain because they use more government services than they pay in taxes. Griswold points out that immigrants tend to be young and healthy and do not rely much on health care and "overcrowding in certain school districts is more likely driven by new births and internal migration than by newly arrived immigrants."[18] By law, illegal immigrants do not have access to unemployment benefits, food stamps, or Medicare. Griswold adds that this assessment also does not take into account that second and third generation descendants typically make more money and achieve a better education than the foreign-born first generation, as determined in data collected by the U.S. Census Bureau.

Access to Healthcare

The immediate impact of immigration is most often dealt with by communities on the local level. Copper Queen Hospital in Bisbee, AZ, approximately 10 miles (16 km) north of the south-

The National Council of La Raza

NCLR, commonly referred to as La Raza, a term which means "the race" in English, is largest organization in the United States dedicated exclusively to Hispanic civil rights and advocacy:

> Through its network of nearly 300 affiliated community-based organizations, NCLR reaches millions of Hispanics each year in 41 states, Puerto Rico, and the District of Columbia.

> NCLR serves all Hispanic nationality groups in all regions of the country through its formal network of nearly 300 Affiliates and a broader network of more than 35,000 groups and individuals nationwide – reaching millions of Hispanics annually. NCLR welcomes affiliation from independent Hispanic groups that share

NCLR's goals and self-help philosophy. NCLR also assists Hispanic groups that are not formal Affiliates through issue networks on health, education, housing, leadership, and other issue areas.

NCLR has produced and offers a range of resources to educate the public and the Latino community about important issues. In particular, its publications are a credible source of facts and information on a wide range of issues, from education and health to political and social empowerment. They present a uniquely Hispanic perspective, particularly on issues affecting minority, limited-English-speaking, and/or low-income Hispanics.

National Council of La Raza Web site, http://www.nclr.org/section/about/mission

ern U.S. border, is the only hospital for many miles and often receives patients who have been injured illegally crossing the border. The $3,000 to $4,000 in free care Copper Queen administers to illegal immigrants each month have compelled it to close other services, including obstetrics, forcing local residents to travel as far as 100 miles (160km) for prenatal care.

A PATH TO CITIZENSHIP?

"They want to pay taxes because they want to be here and stay here and become U.S. citizens. They'll do whatever it takes, and they think it looks better on their behalf if they can prove they paid taxes. They think it will help them get some kind of permanent residency."

Luis Diaz, director of Progreso Latino, a service organization for the Latino community, quoted in Summer Harlow, "Filing taxes seen as path to citizenship," *Wilmington News Journal,* April 17, 2007.

Montgomery County, Pennsylvania, introduced a controversial prenatal care program that targets illegal immigrants who cannot afford health care. Supporters of this program believe that it makes better sense to ensure that children are born healthy and do not require more expensive medical services later in life. "Deportation is not in our domain," states county human services Director Joseph Roynan. "Our domain is the care of infants, to make as sure as possible that they are not born with birth defects or other disabilities regardless of the status of the infant's mother."[19]

Opponents of this policy like East Norristown, PA, resident Ruth Miller accuse county officials of facilitating illegal immigration. "Before that child is born, the mother is here illegally and should be deported."[20] People who share this sentiment have also voiced concern that illegal immigrants are deliberately creating an opportunity to remain in the United States by having children here because federal law mandates that any child born on American soil is automatically an American citizen, regardless of the citizenship status of the parents. Such children are nicknamed "anchor babies" because their illegal immigrant parents can avoid deportation in order to care for their American child, thus creating a reason, or "anchor," for them to remain.

Access to Education

Impassioned arguments are also taking place over whether illegal immigrants should have access to education, particularly at the college level. Texas and several other states have passed laws in recent years that allow illegal immigrants to pay in-state tuition rates to state universities if they graduated from high school or received a General Equivalency Development (GED) degree in the state. This law has allowed illegal immigrants to also receive financial aid that they would otherwise be denied.

Opinions are divided on the issue of whether illegal immigrants should have access to education, particularly at the college level.

In 2007, Texas State Representative Jim Jackson proposed a bill that would deny in-state tuition rates to applicants who could not prove legal residency, forcing them to pay substantially higher out-of-state fees. "The bottom line is it doesn't make sense to most people in my district, in my opinion, that those who are in the country illegally would be getting a special benefit over others," says Jackson.[21]

It is unclear how many illegal immigrants have taken advantage of Texas's in-state rate provision, and if it truly puts native-born college applicants at a disadvantage, but educated estimates believe that a few hundred to a couple of thousand illegal immigrants are paying in-state tuition out of a statewide enrollment of 120,000. Supporters of the current rate scheme believe that since the state government has already paid for public school education for these students, it should follow through on the investment it has made to educate them and help them better their lives. "Texas would be eating its seed corn [by reversing the tuition law], and that's not a Texas value," says State Representative Rick Noriega.[22]

Paying Taxes

Opponents of allowing illegal immigrants access to government services like health care and education worry that the cost of these services is not being covered by the taxes that they pay, giving them an unfair advantage in access to services paid for primarily by native-born and legal immigrant taxpayers. Steven Camarota, director of research for the Center for Immigration Studies, an organization dedicated to immigration reform, noted, "On average, the costs that illegal immigrant households impose on federal coffers are less than half that of other households, but their tax payments are only one-fourth that of other households."[23]

Supporters disagree with this notion, referring to the concept that allowing illegal immigrants access to social services is essentially making an investment in their current needs that will be paid back in the future through these immigrants' greater prosperity. They also claim that more illegal immigrants are paying taxes than in the past because they are hoping to establish a paper trail that could one day lead to citizenship.

"I feel it's my responsibility to pay," says Queens, NY, construction worker Dionicio Quinde Lima, an illegal immigrant. "And if it helps me get papers, fine."[24] Lima and millions like him file income taxes with the Internal Revenue Service (IRS) with a taxpayer identification number that the IRS gives out to encourage noncitizens to pay their taxes. Since the numbers were introduced in 1996, 11 million have been issued to illegal immigrants. In 2005, 1.9 million tax returns were filed using these numbers, up 30 percent from 2004 and suggesting that more illegal immigrants are filling.

FILING FOR THE REFUND

"First of all, almost all the people filing tax returns are doing it because they're going to get tax refunds. It's a bad thing, because they're not obeying the law—they're deciding which laws they prefer to obey. If they were interested in demonstrating their law-abiding nature, they would pack up and go home."

Mark Krikorian, director of Center for Immigration Studies, a policy organization. Quoted in Nina Bernstein, "Tax Returns Rise for Immigrants in U.S. Illegally," *New York Times,* April 16, 2007.

The IRS does not ask about citizenship status and does not share its information with other agencies. "We want your money whether you are here legally or not," states IRS Commissioner Mark W. Everson, "and whether you earned it legally or not."[25]

Camarota is not impressed by the recent surge in tax filings, pointing out that this does not necessarily mean that illegal immigrants are paying their fair share of taxes, stating, "Illegals are smart enough to know if they owe taxes, they won't file a return."[26]

Opponents of this view note that illegal immigrants are not able to avoid their tax responsibility as many would believe, pointing out that they pay sales taxes on goods and services like citizens. They have also paid $300 billion into the government Social Security retirement fund between 2000 and 2004 that

they will never be able to withdraw money unless they become citizens, in which case they will be entitled to the benefits they have paid. This concerns some lawmakers because the Social Security fund is expected to run dangerously low in the next decade with the impending retirement of 70 million Baby Boomers. They maintain the additional withdrawals from one-time illegal immigrants that were not calculated into the fund's disbursement could further drain the Social Security fund.

Of further concern to lawmakers are the rising remittances, or cash payments, legal and illegal immigrants send to relatives back home. Hispanic immigrants sent $62 billion to their native countries in 2006, 14 percent more than in 2005, and four times as much money as was sent from 1994 to 2004. Mexico alone received $23 billion, enough to make remittances the third largest component of their economy after oil and tourism. Critics of immigration resent remittances because it amounts to money taken directly out of the U.S. economy for the benefit of other nations. Many in the United States business community, however, believe that legal and illegal immigrants are more of a benefit to the American economy.

The Growing Hispanic Market in the United States

The large number of Hispanic immigrants in America has brought with it exciting opportunities for companies looking to expand their consumer reach and increase their profits. In 2006 Hispanic consumers added $700 billion to the U.S. economy. A Hispanic/Latino market profile conducted by Magazine Publishers of America in March 2007 stated that the spending power of the Hispanic community could reach $1.2 trillion by 2001, a rise of 457 percent from 1990 that represents the fastest growing segment of the economy. Hispanic-owned businesses in the United States are growing three times faster than the national average, and the total Hispanic market in this country ranks as

OPPOSITE: *Hispanic-owned businesses are growing rapidly in the United States, as are businesses that target the Hispanic market.*

the third largest Hispanic economy in the world, followed only by the nations of Brazil and Mexico.

The desire for goods and services as well as media entertainment in the Hispanic community has driven American companies to create consumer products and content that caters exclusively to its taste. Advertising on Spanish language television was a $3 billion business in 2005, and Latinvox is one company that has benefited from the growth of the Hispanic market. Founded in 2002 by Roberto Ramos and Susan Jaramillo, immigrants from Cuba and Venezuela, respectively, Latinvox is an advertising and business-consulting agency that has grown more than 100 percent in the past four years.

The success of Latinvox and other Hispanic-owned businesses has far reaching implications not only for the U.S. economy but also for the Western Hemisphere as a whole. As U.S. Hispanics further establish their business presence in this country, their success will filter back to their country of origin, notes Eric Farnsworth, vice president of the Washington-based Council of the Americas, an advocacy group for businesses throughout the Western Hemisphere. This will strengthen the economic links between the U.S. Hispanic market and the rest of the hemisphere creating a strong entrepreneurial group and a wider base of intellectual capital in the Western Hemisphere. [27]

Taking Jobs Americans Don't Want

Immigrants rarely come to America to be idle, which fits well in a country that has always taken pride in a strong work ethic that rewards those willing to exert themselves. The latest wave of immigrants, though controversial in many respects, could not have come at a better time in America's economic development. Rising GDP, low unemployment, and the expanding markets of the global economy have created numerous opportunities for business owners and workers alike, and immigrants stand to benefit greatly from the prosperity.

Hispanic immigrants have met the demand for low-skilled labor that the United States currently needs. The U.S. Labor Department states that of the top 20 jobs with the largest expected

Hispanic immigrants are meeting the demand for low-skilled labor in the United States. These jobs are typically in the service industry and include retail sales, food preparation, landscaping, janitors, and home aids.

growth between 2002 and 2012, 14 require "short-term-on-the-job" training. These jobs are typically in the service industry and include retail sales, food preparation, landscaping, janitors, and home aids. Net growth in this sector is expected to exceed five million in the next decade. This trend matches well with the native population, which is growing older and more educated, as the median age of American workers is rising and more are attaining college degrees than ever before in the nation's history. These older and more educated workers are less likely to pursue low-wage jobs in the service sector that immigrants readily accept.

There is a concern, however, for the many native-born low-skilled workers who could effectively be priced out of the job market by immigrants who are willing to work longer hours at tougher jobs for less money. "Even in the sector of the economy in which illegal immigrants have the highest representation—agriculture—they are just 24 percent of the workers," writes columnist Thomas Sewell. "Where did the other 76 percent come from, if these are jobs that Americans won't do?"[28]

Griswold argues that the direct competition between natives and immigrants in certain sectors of the job market is offset by the lower prices for goods and services that come as a result of immigration. Americans also benefit from "opportunities created for more skilled native-born workers in those industries that depend on immigrant workers to meet the needs of their customers."[29]

UNDOCUMENTED CHILDREN

"I understand these students are not responsible for their undocumented status, having come to the United States with their parents. The fact remains, however, that these students and their parents are here illegally and neither sympathy nor good intentions can ameliorate that fact."

Connecticut Governor Jodi Rell. Quoted in Gregory B. Hladky, "Rell Vetoes Bill to Give Undocumented Children In-State Rates for College," *New Haven (Connecticut) Register,* June 27, 2007.

The full impact legal and illegal immigrant labor has on the ability of native-born Americans to get work is hard to gauge, since there is no way to accurately determine who does not get a particular job as opposed to how many jobs have been filled. However, there is little disagreement that companies will more readily hire workers who will work for less money because it means larger profit margins. It is also well established that immigrants who work for less money draw down real wages in certain industries which has drawn the anger of many working class citizens and labor unions that seek to protect workers' wages and benefits. Justich and Ng noted in their report for Bear Stearns that, "The large infusion of the imported labor supply has reduced average annual wage earnings by approximately 4 to 6 percent."[30]

Illegal immigrants will readily work for less money because it is still more than they would receive for the same work in their native countries. However, they are often taken advantage of by dishonest companies that capitalize on the fact that these workers often do not know the rights and benefits that all workers are entitled to by U.S. law, and do not report abuses for fear of being deported. These companies sometimes find workers through equally unprincipled labor brokers who seek out the illegal immigrants and take part of their salary as a fee for finding them the job. "The [guest worker] program has been rife with abuses, even during the best of times," says Cindy Hahamovitch, a history professor at the College of William and Mary who is writing a book on immigrant workers in the United States "There will never be enough inspectors to check every labor camp, contract and field."[31]

Companies can only be penalized for hiring illegal workers if they knowingly do so, which is difficult for prosecutors to prove when a labor broker is involved because the company can claim that it is the responsibility of the broker to establish a worker's citizenship status. This type of behavior is quite common in the construction industry, where many companies work through labor brokers.

Hispanics filled two out of every three new jobs in construction in 2006, accounting for 372,000 out of the 559,000 jobs created. Their contribution to the industry is evident in these numbers, but labor advocates have cited a high level of abuse. "These companies are getting rich on the backs of undocumented workers," notes Gustavo Maldonado, a local union organizer with the Carpenters' District Council of Kansas City & Vicinity. "The workers are seen as the problem, but it's the companies that lure them to these construction jobs, pay them cash, or not pay them at all. It's not fair to the industry, and it's not fair to the workers."[32]

Construction companies, as well as companies in other industries who rely on cheap illegal immigrant labor, reduce their costs by not offering wage and health benefits and by classifying their workers as independent contractors which allows them to

avoid checking immigration status and paying payroll taxes and workers compensation. Additionally, legitimate businesses are at a disadvantage because companies that do not pay these benefits can offer their services at a lower price to public and private sector customers.

In 2006, the federal government began cracking down on companies that knowingly hired illegal immigrants. Alex Salaiz, district director of the U.S. Department of Labor's Wage and Hour Division in Denver, states that it is not unreasonable to monitor every employer, but the Labor Department needs more resources in order to combat the problem. "We do the best with the resources we have."[33]

THE DESIRE TO SUCCEED

"We're not talking about someone who just stepped off a bus and is asking for favorable treatment. We're talking about young students who exhibit the best of what we expect from all of our children: academic success and the desire to succeed even more."

Connecticut State Senator Donald E. Williams Jr. Quoted in Stacy Stowe, "Bill Giving Illegal Residents Connecticut Tuition Rates Is Vetoed by the Governor," New York Times, June 27, 2007.

Highly publicized raids performed by Immigration and Customs Enforcement (ICE) in late 2006 and early 2007 have led to arrest and deportation hearings for hundreds of illegal immigrants, but employers are now facing criminal penalties for hiring them. Francesco Insolia, owner of Michael Bianco, Inc., a textile company in New Bedford, MA, has been accused of exploiting workers with low wages and deplorable working conditions. Melvin McKay, president of California based Golden State Fence, a company contracted to help build a border fence to keep illegal immigrants from entering the United States, was fined $200,000 and sentenced to community service for hiring illegal immigrants.

OPPOSITE: *Companies that knowingly hire illegal immigrants face criminal penalties if caught. Pictured here is the Immigration and Customs Enforcement (ICE) raid at Michael Bianco Inc., which employed hundreds of illegal workers.*

The trend toward punishing employers is widely believed by immigration reform advocates to help deter illegal immigration. If American companies face huge fines and the potential loss of their business, they will not so readily hire illegal immigrants, which will dry up the job opportunities available. Those who continue to defend the hiring of illegal immigrants state that the low wages they accept keep consumer prices down and generate healthy profits for American companies. While that mentality persists, policing the border will remain a difficult and expensive task.

The Cost of Policing the Border

Illegal immigration laws in the United States went largely unenforced for many years. The number of people picked up illegally crossing the border was small in comparison to those who actually got through, and 98 percent of those arrested between 2000 and 2005 were never prosecuted, according to an Associated Press analysis of federal data. The lax security at the border has been of great concern since the terrorist attacks of September 11, 2001, when close to 3,000 people were killed by Islamic terrorists who hijacked passenger planes and crashed them into New York City's World Trade Center, the Pentagon in Washington, DC, and a field near Shanksville, Pennsylvania. When it was revealed that the nineteen terrorists responsible for the attack were all living in the United States illegally with expired student visas, it became apparent that America's immigration system was broken to the point of being a threat to national security. Policing the southern border to prevent future attacks on American soil became a high priority for law enforcement.

With increased calls for security at the southern border, the federal government is now trying to play catch-up. The Department of Homeland Security (DHS) initiated a plan in 2006 to add 6,000 agents to the U.S. Customs and Border Patrol (CBP) through 2009. It costs $187,744 to hire and train each new agent that is brought in to help police the 2,000-mile (3,218 km) border. While this training is taking place, 6,000 U.S. Army National Guard soldiers will be deployed along the border to make up for the shortfall in manpower necessary to control illegal border crossings.

Recognizing that the border is too long to be watched by human eyes alone, the federal government has begun the Secure Border Initiative (SBInet), which will include fencing, vehicle barriers, motion sensors, cameras, and radar to monitor the region. SBInet, which is slated for completion by 2011, will carry a price tag of $7.6 billion. "With manpower and technology, you can bring the border under control," notes Border Patrol supervisor Randy Clark.[34]

SBInet is not foolproof, though. The harsh environmental conditions of the desert through which the border stretches have caused electrical shorts in cameras and motion sensors. The

In the wake of the September 11, 2001, terrorist attacks against the United States, tightened security along the 2000-mile U.S.–Mexico border has become a high priority.

fence is an obstacle that can be surmounted with a ladder that costs $5 on the Mexican side of the border, and an internal audit by DHS revealed that the 11,000 sensors already in place have accounted for less than 1 percent of border apprehensions.

The illegal immigrants who are arrested need to be processed and incarcerated, which also costs more money than has been allocated in the past. Operation Streamline, a CBP project to arrest and convict rather than deport illegal border crossers, has swamped courts in the Southwest with immigration-related cases. New Mexico handled 397 such cases in 2006, compared to the national average of 84. Martha Vazquez, chief judge for the District of New Mexico, was prompted to ask of the CBP,

A U.S. Border Patrol agent monitors the U.S–Mexico border at night with the use of infrared cameras.

"Do you realize that the second week into this we're going to run out of (jail) space?"[35]

California received $85 million from the federal government in 2005 to offset the cost of apprehending and incarcerating illegal immigrants. This was the highest amount allocated to any state that year due to California's high percentage of illegal immigrants, but all states have expended some level of financial resources to combat the illegal immigrant problem and they have called upon the federal government to pick up more of the cost of incarcerating illegal immigrants. The White House Office of Management and Budget, however, proposed eliminating the program to reimburse state and local governments because "It has no criminal justice goals and cannot demonstrate results."[36]

This action by the White House leaves open the debate about what level of responsibility for controlling immigration lies with the federal government and what lies with the states. There is also a debate about whether the responsibility of assimilation of immigrants into American society lies with Americans or with the immigrants themselves.

CHAPTER 4

ASSIMILATION AND IDENTITY

The most attractive aspect of America being a "nation of immigrants" is that both citizens as well as foreign-born newcomers benefit from living together in the United States. Throughout American history, immigrants gained access to the country's vast economic resources and were given the opportunity to immeasurably improve their lives. A great cultural adaptation took place when immigrants became a part of the country's rich democratic and cultural heritage. Native-born Americans gained the opportunity to similarly enrich their own lives by being exposed to the multitude of cultures that immigrants added to America by learning about the foreign lands of these immigrants that they might not otherwise learn about without traveling abroad. While the elements of this cultural exchange have changed over time with the addition of immigrants from different nations, the principles of freedom, democracy, and individualism upon which the nation was founded remain unchanged.

BRINGING MEXICO TO AMERICA

"Some of those that come to this country from Mexico aren't interested in assimilation. They're interested in bringing Mexico to this country. I think when people come to this country they should be interested in assimilation."

U.S. Rep. Virgil Goode (R-VA) Quoted in Shawn Hopkins, "Goode: President Wrong on Immigration," *Martinsville (Virginia) Bulletin*, June 18, 2007.

Immigrants were expected to adopt and preserve these principles as well as learn the English language and American customs in a process called assimilation. "Immigrants were expected only to abide by the basic tenets of an unspoken 'assimilation contract': allegiance to the nation's democratic principles, respect for individualism and hard work and—yes—willingness to learn English and use it outside their homes," writes Peter D. Salins, professor of political science at the State University of New York, Stony Brook, in Reinventing the Melting Pot. "Beyond that, they were free to indulge ethnic, cultural or religious preferences and practices to their hearts' content."[37]

Fears in the past that the assimilation contract that Salins refers to would be broken proved to be unfounded. Immigrants from many nations went on to become upstanding American cit-

The Cost of Illegal Immigration in New York State

The Federation for American Immigration Reform (FAIR), a public interest group dedicated to the issue of immigration reform, undertakes numerous research projects to measure the impact of illegal immigration in the United States The following is from a report entitled "The Cost of Illegal Immigration to New Yorkers":

> In 2005, some 645,000 illegal aliens were estimated to live in New York. Education represents the largest single component of New York's illegal alien fiscal liability about $4.3 billion a year. Statewide, FAIR estimates about 120,000 children are in the country illegally and an additional 225,000 are children born here to illegal aliens. Combined, these students represent 11.7 percent of public school kids. Publicly funded health care for illegal aliens costs the state about $690 million a year, while illegal aliens in state prisons drain another $165 million from state coffers. The typical native-headed household in New York pays an estimated $874 a year in taxes to cover the costs of just these three programs...

> FAIR's 2005 estimate of $5.1 billion means that the costs of illegal immigration have more than doubled in just 11 years.

Federation for American Immigration Reform Web site, http://www.fairus.org/site/PageServer?pagename=media_release9202006

izens, even when certain native groups treated them with prejudice and attempted to prevent them from obtaining the rights of
citizens. The Latin American immigrant wave represents a challenge to this longstanding practice of assimilation. Opponents
of open immigration fear that the large numbers of Hispanics
coming to the United States and the prominence of Hispanic
culture in this country will not assimilate and will instead remain a separate culture with a separate language, fracturing the
unified national identity. Opponents further believe that some
Americans are discouraging assimilation by immigrants because
they feel ethnic heritage is more important than American pa-
triotism.

Supporters of immigration maintain that Hispanic immigrants will assimilate in time like all immigrants before them,
and that it is too early to accuse them of breaking the assimilation contract. Furthermore, immigration supporters believe it
is native-born Americans who are in danger of breaking that
contract if they push too hard for assimilation.

The Evolving American Identity

"Historically the substance of American identity has involved
four key components: race, ethnicity, culture (most notably
language and religion), and ideology," writes Harvard professor
Samuel P. Huntington in his book *Who Are We? The Challenges to
America's National Identity*.[38] While America's heritage of free en-
terprise and democracy and its cultural language component of
English remained unchanged throughout its history, the racial,
ethnic, and religious elements have evolved over many years.

The American identity at the time of the Declaration of Independence could be described as white western European and
Protestant. This remained unchanged until after the Civil War,
when two significant developments took place. Freed slaves
were guaranteed basic civil rights by law, although institution-
alized racism and segregation in the form of poll taxes, voting
restrictions, and separate educational and health facilities kept
blacks from being truly equal for more than a century. Also,
the addition of Catholics and Jews migrating from Ireland and

*Many people agree that a balance must be maintained between immigrants'
adoption of American culture and the preservation of their native culture. Pictured
here is the Hispanic celebration* quinceanera, *which marks a young woman's 15th
birthday.*

Eastern and Southern Europe and immigrants from Asia began
to change the religious, racial, and ethnic composition of the
country. Though America remains 77 percent white in its racial
composition, the evolution of its identity continues to this day.

Huntington, a strong voice among opponents of open immigration, argues that the American identity has not evolved but it
has been deliberately changed in favor of a multicultural American identity: "[Supporters of open immigration] encouraged immigrants to maintain their birth country cultures, granted them
legal privileges denied to native-born Americans, and denounced
the idea of Americanization as un-American."[39] In Huntington's
view, the multiculturalism that these deconstructionists are trying to achieve will ultimately harm America's identity because

it divides people. It does not offer the opportunity for celebrating the shared link of one overarching American identity, but instead encourages ethnic groups to derive strength from their differences.

THE PUSH TO NATURALIZE

"Many of these people, they have been here for years and years. Some people, they came when they were 2 years old and they never decided to become American. ... With all these anti-immigrant propositions and all the proposals coming, they want to vote."

Reyna Polanco, an organizer with the Arizona Coalition for Migrant Rights. Quoted in Mike Madden, "Backlash Fears Drive Efforts to Naturalize," *Arizona Republic*, February 23, 2007.

Stanford University political science professor Luis R. Fraga and University of Washington political science professor Gary M. Segura refuted Huntington's views and were prompted to ask, "How important is a single national culture for the preservation of democratic institutions?"[40] In their view multiculturalism gives groups the ability to maintain their ethnic and cultural heritage. They also cite examples of what they believe are successful democracies that have substantial ethnic and language diversity in Spain, France, and India. However, each of these nations has suffered recent political strife among various ethnic or religious groups that has led to violence: Spain has been engaged in a decades-long conflict with Basque separatists, France experienced violent riots in 2006 started by Islamic fundamentalists in the suburbs of Paris, and India has a history of religious conflict between Hindus and Muslims.

Huntington fears that America's future will include the same conflicts that these nations experience if it continues on the path of embracing a multicultural identity. It is doubtful that America's identity could become similarly divided because immigrants readily adopt American values, sometimes without even realizing it. Boston College political science professor Peter Skerry notes one such example. "Villagers from Mexico, Guatemala, Columbia and other Spanish-speaking countries do not come to the United States thinking of themselves as 'Hispanics' or 'Latinos.' That is an identity they acquire on these shores."[41] In other words, according to Skerry, people who make up the Hispanic community in the United States only think of themselves as Hispanic because they are in America. They campaign for civil rights and fair treatment in America based on an identity they embrace that is unique in this country.

Despite their differing views on the virtues of the American identity in an age of multiculturalism, opponents of open immigration like Huntington and supporters of open immigration like Fraga and Segura do share a concern for the American identity to remain intact and evolve in a way that benefits all Americans, immigrants and native-born alike. A balance must be maintained between the adoption of American culture and the preservation of the cultural elements brought by immigrants from their native lands.

Are Hispanic Immigrants Assimilating?

It is difficult to determine whether recent Hispanic immigrants are actually assimilating into American society, because assimilation is a process that takes place over generations and many immigrants have not been in this country long enough to be fully assimilated. Assimilation or lack of it can only be determined by comparatively measuring, among other things, the extent of English language usage and the economic status of American-born children and grandchildren compared to

Many U.S. cities with large Hispanic populations post signs that are written in both English and Spanish.

that of their immigrant ancestors. Supporters of open immigration believe that for opponents like Huntington to argue that Hispanics are not assimilating is not only to be a premature assumption, but also a false one. According to Gregory Rodriguez, writer and senior fellow of the New America Foundation, a pro-immigration group, Mexican-Americans have not attempted to build a parallel ethnic institutional structure, "Nor have Mexican Americans ever shown much interest in distancing themselves from the mainstream.... For example, in Los Angeles, home to more Mexicans than any other city in the U.S., there is not one ethnic Mexican hospital, college, cemetery or broad-based charity."[42]

The concern Huntington and other opponents of open immigration express about the perceived lack of Hispanic assimilation was commonly voiced in the past when large waves of German immigrants came to America in the nineteenth century. According to the 2000 Census, the Hispanic population in the United States was 35.3 million, or 12.5 percent of the total U.S. population. By way of comparison, the number of people who claimed German ancestry in the 2000 Census was 42.8 million, or 15.2 percent of the total population. Germans living in America and Americans of German ancestry clearly outnumber Hispanics, yet there is no concern voiced by Huntington or any other advocates of controlled immigration about the high proportion of German-Americans in the United States. While much is heard about the issues and concerns of the Hispanic community, there is no vocal German-American lobby that is petitioning for German rights, and there are no German-American leaders advocating German issues. Politicians and the media do not speak of the German vote, where Democrats and Republicans alike covet the Hispanic vote.

Harvard history professor Stephan Thernstrom maintains that the reason there is no German-American community that compares to the Hispanic-American community in terms of political action and visibility is because Germans have assimilated into the American culture. "There was a German ethnic group once, a huge and powerful one," Thernstrom writes. "But having [ancestors] from Germany is not a significant indicator of how these people live and how they think of themselves."[43] During the high point of German immigration in the late 1800s, schools in Milwaukee, WI, which had the highest concentration of German immigrants in the country, taught students in German as well as English. Today there are sizable German-American communities in cities across the United States, and there are festivals and parades in each of those cities that celebrate the German heritage; however, that heritage is no longer the defining element of Americans of German descent living in the United States today.

AMERICA IS NOT BECOMING A SPANISH-SPEAKING NATION

"The United States is not becoming a Spanish-speaking nation.... the facts do not support the increasing public image that millions of immigrants refuse to learn or speak English or do not want to assimilate."

Roberto Calderin, past chairman of the Orange County, New York, Human Rights Commission. *Times Herald-Record (Middletown, NY)*, October 5, 2006.

The circumstances regarding the Hispanic immigration experience in America are different than they were for Germans or any other ethnic or national group in the past. Hispanic immigrants are arriving in America in numbers that dwarf any previous immigration wave, and they are coming faster than the federal government can process their naturalization and citizenship requests. This, and the long unwatched border that America shares with Mexico, facilitates a high level of illegal immigration by people who do not want to wait in line for permission to enter the United States and, instead, simply walk into the country. In the past, immigrants had to cross an ocean by boat to come to America.

The great difference between the Mexican and American economies combined with their geographical status as neighbors with a land border creates another reason for immigration that is unique in the history of American immigration. "The income gap between the United States and Mexico is the largest between two [neighboring] countries in the world," writes historian David Kennedy.[44]

Hispanic immigrants tend to concentrate in certain areas; California, New York, Texas, and Florida are the destinations of choice because they already have large Hispanic populations. Ethnic enclaves, which are communities made up of distinct ethnic groups, are not unique in the immigrant experience, since strangers in a strange land will often gravitate toward what is familiar in order to feel safer. However, no other immigration wave has had such a high percentage of people who speak the same language, and the large populations in the Hispanic enclaves adds to the concern that assimilation will be slowed or will not take place at all.

People concerned with the lack of assimilation among Hispanic immigrants believe that within these tight-knit communities where all the basic necessities of life can be provided by familiar faces speaking Spanish, there is little need to reach out and interact with the broader American population. Proof of this can be found in the drop in marriages between Hispanics and whites between 1990 and 2000, which is likely because of the continuous arrival of more immigrants from Latin America, allowing Hispanics to reinforce their cultural identity. The regional concentration of Hispanic immigrants may be changing, though, as statisticians have noted that immigrants have been dispersing to other areas within the last couple of years, suggesting that Hispanic immigrants are integrating into and becoming accepted in traditionally native-born American communities.

A further positive sign that assimilation may actually be taking place, even if it is at a slower rate than in previous immigration waves is the rising level of American identity among Hispanics. A 2002 Pew Research Center survey which inquired how Hispanics preferred to identify themselves revealed that while only 7 percent of foreign-born Hispanics identified themselves first as Americans, 31 percent of second generation Hispanics and 56 percent of third generation Hispanics identified themselves primarily as American.

The Rush to Become a Citizen

A recent sharp rise in the number of Hispanic immigrants applying for U.S. citizenship in early 2007 may have been motivated more by practical concerns than the desire to assimilate. In January 2007, the U.S. Bureau of Citizenship and Immigration Services (CIS) announced that it would be raising the application fees for citizenship and green cards in six months' time, setting off a rush of applications by immigrants from all nations. In June, green cards went from $325 to $905, and green cards holders who wanted to become citizens were required to pay $595, up from $330. The fee hikes came in advance of new federal budget proposals that required CIS to pay 99 percent of its 2008 budget (an estimated $2.6 billion) with money made from 2007 application fees. The increase in application fees was also made to cover the cost of hiring more staff and upgrading facilities so that CIS could reduce the application backlog that dates back several years.

Kevin Appleby, spokesman for the U.S. Conference of Catholic Bishops, which provides services for refugees and migrants,

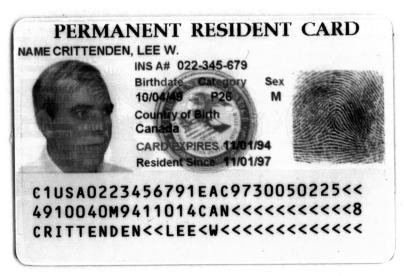

Permanent Resident Cards, known as "green cards," are issued to lawful permanent residents as evidence of their authorization to live and work in the United States.

noted, "There are some who will struggle to pay (the fee increase). A lot of migrants have other expenses to survive."[45]

Rick Hogan, a Wilmington, DE, immigration attorney disagrees. "They'll pay it because it's the best investment they will make. They'll work extra if they have to because they are eager to be here."[46]

SPANISH IS EVERYWHERE

"You're just forced to speak English, and that just makes you learn the language faster. It is much more difficult and much more challenging when you are ... let's say, Latino. Because you have so many Latinos, as I see at the Capitol in Sacramento, there are so many Latinos who speak Spanish all the time, they speak to each other in Spanish. So it makes it difficult to perfect their English skills as quickly as possible."

California Governor Arnold Schwarzenegger, quoted in Kevin Yamamura, "Schwarzenegger: Hispanics Should Shun Spanish Media to Learn English," *Scripps News*, June 14, 2007.

Applications in January 2007 were up 81 percent over January 2006, to 95,076. Many of those applications were filed by immigrants motivated over fears about the outcome of immigration reform being debated by legislators in Washington, DC. "You hear so many things on the news," admitted Jeaneth Romero, a pre-school teacher in Arizona. "Maybe tomorrow, they're going to pass a new law that says they're not going to allow any more people here or they're not going to allow me to become a citizen, so I better apply."[47]

Aside from beating the clock on higher fees and new laws, the Pew Research Center released a report in 2007 that the proportion of legal foreign-born residents who became naturalized U.S. citizens reached 52 percent in 2005, or 12.8 million people. This is the highest level in 25 years and a 15 percent increase since 1990, when the percentage of naturalizations reached an historic low. An additional 8 million immigrants were eligible for naturalization in 2005, with Mexicans comprising more than a third of that number.

Many adult education programs offer English language classes for people who have immigrated to the United States.

Learning the National Language

While Mexicans have a comparatively lower tendency toward naturalization than other immigrant groups, by and large they are following traditional patterns of absorbing the English language. Generally, immigrants follow a pattern in which the foreign-born first generation overwhelmingly speaks the native language while having little mastery of English. The second generation demonstrates a mastery of English and is generally bilingual (speak both English and their native language), and the third generation speaks English almost exclusively with little if any use of their native language. A study of two decades' worth of census data by University of California, Berkeley professors Jack Citrin, Amy Lerman, Michael Murakami, and University of Minnesota professor Kathryn Pearson determined that "Mexican immigrants may know less English than newcomers from other countries when they arrived in the United States, but…their rate

of linguistic assimilation [the rate at which they learn English] is on par with or greater than those of other contemporary immigrant groups."[48]

According to the 2000 Census 43 percent of first generation Mexicans spoke only Spanish at home, and 73.6 percent did not speak English very well. The second generation demonstrated a marked improvement in English language ability, with 11.6 percent speaking only Spanish or more Spanish than English, 25 percent speaking Spanish and English equally, and 30.1 percent speaking only English. This level of improvement in only one generation shows that there is little need for concern about the prevalence of Spanish-language media and advertising affecting linguistic assimilation in the United States It also comes as welcome news for Hispanics looking to get ahead in the job market. "Hispanic immigrants who speak English earn 17 percent more than those who do not," notes Harvard University professor George J. Borjas, "even after adjusting for differences in education and other socio-economic characteristics between the two groups."[49]

English Education

In order for Hispanic immigrant children to have the tools they need to succeed later in life, it is essential that they learn to speak English proficiently. There is also an ongoing debate as to the best way to teach English to Hispanic students in America's public schools, with supporters of bilingual education squaring off against supporters of English language immersion.

Bilingual education is a program that starts out by teaching elementary school students in their native language, with gradually increased exposure to English as they move through the school system. Supporters of bilingual education claim that it allows children to gain literacy and fundamental knowledge in subjects like math and science in their native language before tackling English literacy and proficiency. It is also believed

OPPOSITE: *Bilingual education is a program that starts out by teaching elementary school students in their native language, with gradually increased exposure to English as they move through the school system.*

that this program avoids subjecting children to the psychological trauma of isolation from their English-speaking classmates and prevents them from getting behind in other school subjects while maintaining cultural ties to their native heritage.

English language immersion is a program in which children are taught English from an early stage in their educational development. They are also instructed in the fundamentals of math and science in English, thereby allowing them to achieve English proficiency at a faster rate. Supporters of English language immersion note that students more readily grasp both English and other subjects, and they assimilate faster than they would with bilingual education.

The California public school system, which has more Hispanic students than any other school system in the country, has experimented with both programs, and there are teachers and parents who passionately support one program or the other. However, a five-year study by the California state legislature found no conclusive evidence that either program was more effective than the other. As with many other aspects of the larger debate on immigration, no single answer can be applied to the entire immigrant community.

CHAPTER
5

CALLS FOR REFORM

It has been more than forty years since the federal government made any fundamental change in immigration policy. The 1965 Immigration and Nationality Act essentially eliminated the national origin quotas that had been in place for decades, and introduced a period of unchecked immigration whose direct result was the dramatic increase of illegal immigration and the widespread use of undocumented laborers. The Immigration Reform and Control Act of 1986 (IRCA) attempted to rectify this situation by criminalizing the hiring of illegal immigrants, but the provisions put in place to punish companies who hired illegals were not enforced. Additionally, the 1986 law gave amnesty to three million illegal immigrants in the United States, which essentially forgave them for breaking the law by entering the country and allowed them to apply for citizenship without any form of punishment or fine.

Modern advocates for the control of immigration look at IRCA as the reason why American immigration policy is in dire need of reform today. These advocates believe that by granting illegal immigrants citizenship, the federal government sent a signal that future illegal border crossers would eventually be rewarded for such behavior. In 2006, members of Congress began work on immigration reform legislation that was geared heavily toward immigration enforcement. Republican lawmakers in the House of Representatives wanted to provide money for hiring more border patrol agents and building physical barriers along the southern border to prevent crossing by illegal immigrants. The bills that were written failed to pass because those who favored immigration were unhappy with the manner in which the illegal immigrant problem and worker visas were handled.

Since then there has been debate about a more comprehensive bill. The demand for stricter enforcement of immigration

Illegal Immigrants Paying Taxes

A point commonly made about illegal immigrants is that they do not pay any taxes and are therefore a drain on government resources. Shikha Dalmia, senior analyst for the Reason Foundation, a policy think tank, points out that this assumption is not correct:

> Close to 8 million of the 12 million or so illegal aliens in the country today file personal income taxes using [IRS issued taxpayer identification] numbers, contributing billions to federal coffers. No doubt they hope that this will one day help them acquire legal status — a plaintive expression of their desire to play by the rules and come out of the shadows.

What's more, aliens who are not self-employed have Social Security and Medicare taxes automatically withheld from their paychecks.

Beyond federal taxes, all illegals automatically pay state sales taxes that contribute toward the upkeep of public facilities such as roads that they use, and property taxes through their rent that contribute toward the schooling of their children. The non-partisan National Research Council found that when the taxes paid by the children of low-skilled immigrant families—most of whom are illegal—are factored in, they contribute on average $80,000 more to federal coffers than they consume.

The Reason Foundation Web site, http://www.reason.org/commentaries/dalmia_20060501.shtml

laws has been matched by concern for the rights of illegal immigrants already in the country. While they should not be rewarded for breaking immigration laws, they should not be punished for simply wanting to come to America to improve their lives. Mass deportation is considered an immoral act because it separates people from their families. It is also unworkable because of the size and scope of the illegal population and the negative effect that plucking 12 to 20 million workers out of their jobs would have on the economy.

Advocates of tighter borders and supporters of illegal immigrants alike have lost patience with the federal government, which only recently moved to combat the problem. States are similarly disappointed with the federal government's lack of leadership on the issue and have begun taking action on their own to address the needs of their respective communities.

Advocacy Groups Make Their Voices Heard

In a democracy such as America's where media attention can be easily drawn, it is not hard for a group to get its message out if it wants to be heard. So it has been with the various political and social leaders in the immigration debate who have sought to influence public opinion and convince lawmakers at the fed-

The issue of immigration in the United States is a complicated one, and groups on both sides of the issue aim to have their views heard as often as possible.

eral level to craft immigration reform to meet their wishes. It will only be known how successful these public campaigns have been when the final immigration reform package is passed by Congress and signed into law by the president. A look at the various issues that are being protested, scrutinized, and dissected does give insight as to which parts may be considered in the overall reform plan.

Unity Blueprint for Immigration Reform

In March 2007, two months before Congress began debating a comprehensive immigration reform package, a coalition of national policy groups, labor unions, activists, and religious and ethnic organizations launched a $4 million national lobbying effort called the Unity Blueprint for Immigration Reform. The Unity Blueprint laid out a series of policy goals that included stronger labor protections and an expansion of permanent worker visas for immigrants, repeal of enforcement measures like penalties against employers of illegal immigrants and the border fence, and a path to legalization for all illegal immigrants in the United States.

THEY CAN DEPORT ANYBODY

"To be honest with you, I'm scared. How can they just pluck me out of my family, my kids? If they can do this to me, they can do it to anybody."

Zoila Meyer, former Adelanto, CA, city councilmember threatened with deportation because she never became a citizen. Quoted in Robert Jablon, "Ex-SoCal Councilwoman Could Be Deported," *Washington Post*, June 24, 2007.

"Civic and labor organizations around the country found themselves on the defensive in 2006, as members of Congress pulled one proposal after another out of their back pocket," said Peter Schey, president of the Los Angeles-based Center for Human Rights and Constitutional Law, an organization that supported the Unity Blueprint. "There was a broad sense of frustration at not having an affirmative position to put forward."[50] The Unity Blueprint was put together in consultation with activ-

The Minuteman Civil Defense Corps, a volunteer group, is dedicated to helping the U.S. Border Patrol watch for illegal immigrants crossing the U.S.–Mexico border.

ists from California, Texas, and Arizona, all states dealing with the illegal immigrant issue.

NumbersUSA and the Minuteman Civil Defense Corp

Groups supporting immigration enforcement have viewed it as a wish list that is totally unworkable. "It's the height of arrogance for someone to come to the U.S., break the law and then ask Congress to overturn or ignore the laws to their benefit," says Caroline Espinosa, spokeswoman for NumbersUSA, a Virginia-based immigration control group.[51]

Another group allied with NumbersUSA is the Minuteman Civil Defense Corps, a volunteer group that gained notoriety in 2005 for carrying out a thirty-day watch at the southern border to watch for illegal immigrants crossing the border. Their purpose was to aid Border Patrol agents who did not have the resources to conduct full sweeps of the border themselves. Minutemen never approached illegal immigrants unless they required medical attention, but would instead inform agents via cell phone of the position of people seen crossing the border. Minuteman chapters have sprung up in several cities across the country, conducting protests against businesses that hire illegal immigrants and counterprotests against immigration advocacy groups. Supporters of immigration enforcement have seen their actions as patriotic, but immigration advocates called them racist.

WE TARGET CRIMINALS

"The people we target are people who have had their day in court. They have final orders but have taken it upon themselves to ignore those orders. These are not random operations. We know exactly who we are looking for."

Lori Haley, spokeswoman for Immigration and Customs Enforcement's western region. Quoted in Leslie Berestein, "Immigration Operation Draws Complaints," *San Diego Union Tribe,* March 28, 2007.

Mike Nava, former Pomona, California Day Labor Center executive director, is one activist who questions the motives of the Minutemen. "They only attend protests that have to do with Mexican or Latino people…you can immediately see that there is a significance of race there because you never see them protesting against any Jewish groups or Irish groups or veterans groups."[52]

Minutemen reject such charges of racism by pointing out that they are protesting the practice of illegal immigration, not the immigrants themselves. The fact that illegal immigrants happen to be predominantly Mexican is incidental. "Our policy as far as hate groups—be it the Nazis, the Ku Klux Klan or unruly Americans—is to not associate with them and distance ourselves from them," says Minuteman spokesman Raymond Herrera. "We are a multiethnic advocacy political group."[53]

The Minuteman group also stirred passions at Columbia University in October 2006 when an appearance by one of their spokesmen prompted several students to storm the stage and disrupt the event. Columbia eventually disciplined those involved and New York City Mayor Michael Bloomberg publicly scolded the University for allowing such an unruly attack on free speech.

Immigration Enforcement

Stricter enforcement of immigration violations by agents of the CBP and ICE has also caused a stir among supporters of open immigration. A renewed focus on enforcement by the federal government and larger operational budgets have given these agencies the resources necessary to conduct raids nationwide in communities where illegal immigrants live. These raids have generated controversy because of the manner in which they are conducted and the results they often yield. Supporters of open immigration suggest that ICE is picking up illegal immigrants at random, while in fact it is actually looking for specific people who have already been to court for immigration violations, skipped their appointed deportation hearings, and become fugitives. Other illegals who represent a priority for ICE are known felons with criminal records.

Nationwide Raids

An ICE search for one illegal immigrant who skipped his deportation hearing led to a raid on a home in East Hampton, NY, in early 2007 which left two terrified children and an angry mother, all naturalized citizens. The suspect was nowhere to be seen. "Your house is supposed to be where you're safe, right?" said Andres Leon, a relative of the family. "When you see police, you're supposed to feel protected. But the way they acted, we don't feel protected; we feel violated."[54]

ICE spokesmen are frequently called upon to explain their tactics to the media, investigators, and attorneys. They defend the actions of their agents by stating that officers are trained to act courteously and with restraint during searches, however they must also perform cautiously for their own safety.

Several East Hampton residents were appalled by the raid, but not everyone was sympathetic. "People here are fed up," said neighbor Richard Herrlin, remarking on the growing presence of illegal immigrants in the community. "It's possible the

Families that contain both legal and illegal immigrants are often separated when an illegal family member is arrested and deported, leaving behind a spouse and children who may legally remain in the United States.

feds showed up because the town officials have done nothing for years, because the town is terrified of being accused of racial insensitivity."[55]

Many other raids that ICE performs have been more successful, resulting in over 18,000 arrests of illegal immigrants in a year's time. One-third of these arrests were classified as collateral, or additional, because they were apprehensions made while agents were seeking other specific individuals. When visiting a suspect's last known address, it is not uncommon for agents to encounter other immigrants who cannot prove their legal status.

Peter Nunez supports the law enforcement effort. Nunez is a former U.S. attorney in San Diego, where a two-week operation in March 2007 resulted in the arrest of 62 fugitives and an additional 297 people who were not targeted, but were determined to be in violation of immigration laws. "If you're going to find one (illegal immigrant), you're going to find a 100."[56]

Deportation

Some advocates for immigrant rights maintain that collateral arrests is just an excuse to conduct mass deportation of hard working people who are immigration violators but do not post a danger to the public. "They're trying to sell it as something where they target (criminals) but it's become part of a larger dragnet," says Pedro Rios, director of the American Friends Service Committee in San Diego.[57]

Immigrant arrests that break up families have also been the focus of concern. The Pew Research Center estimates there are 2.7 million mixed status families in the United States where at least one member is in the country illegally. Raids that round up immigration violators have the potential to take fathers and mothers away from their children and vice versa. In these situations, illegal immigrants have the right to make their circumstances known to immigration judges, who make the final decision about whether or not to deport individuals. Due to an extensive case backlog, potential deportees can remain in legal limbo for months, which creates an agonizing emotional situation while their fates are decided.

Immigration enforcement agents have tried to alleviate the backlog of cases by speeding up the deportation proceedings of some illegals. As part of Operation Return to Sender, ICE's nationwide program for rounding up immigration violators, illegal immigrants in custody may waive their rights to a court hearing and be deported without waiting to see a judge. The wait for a court appearance averages two months, during which time the defendant must remain in jail.

Immigration advocates have received reports from illegal immigrants in custody that agents are pressuring them to sign the waivers and telling them that the wait to see a judge could last several months and will result in deportation anyway. ICE maintains that they are simply offering all the options available to defendants. Barbara Gonzalez, a Miami spokeswoman for U.S. Immigration and Customs Enforcement, says, "Those arrested by ICE officers are afforded with due process of law. Every person in ICE custody receives a `know your rights presentation' and is advised of their rights under U.S. immigration laws."[58]

By definition, all illegal immigrants have in fact broken the law because they are violators of immigration regulations. The first act they committed in the United States was an illegal one because they did not follow the stated procedure for entering the country. However, since the vast majority of illegal immigrants are otherwise law-abiding people whose only desire is to find better jobs than were available in their native countries, many supporters of immigration are willing to forgive their violations. They also do not see the reason for the nationwide sweeps being conducted by ICE. In their view, if immigrants are working hard and obeying the law, they should be afforded the rights available to American citizens because they are contributing to the prosperity of the American economy and should be allowed to reap the benefits of their labor.

Native-born Americans, public officials, and law enforcement officers who want to see immigration laws enforced without prejudice reject the idea that illegal immigrants should be afforded the rights of citizens, because they are not citizens. Pro-immigration-control groups believe it is unfair to allow illegal immigrants the same opportunities available to legal immigrants and citizens who have obeyed all the laws, including immigration regulations. By not exacting some form of punishment for breaking the law, the behavior of illegals is actually being rewarded. This sends what amounts to an open invitation for people in other countries who are contemplating illegal entry into the United States. It also cheapens the value of citizenship that many foreign-born Americans have struggled to legally obtain. Future generations of immigrants will come to realize that if the same result can be achieved without the work, then there is no reason to exert themselves by applying for legal entry.

These views are not lost on lawmakers in Washington, DC, whose recent attempts to craft comprehensive immigration reform have sought to balance the concerns made public by advocates for immigrant rights with the groups calling for greater immigration enforcement.

A U.S. Immigration and Customs Enforcement (ICE) agent takes a suspected illegal immigrant into custody after a raid on a home in 2006.

An Attempt at Federal Reform

In May 2007, the U.S. Congress began debate on the Secure Borders, Economic Opportunity and Immigration Reform Act, a comprehensive immigration reform bill that included provi-

Worksite Enforcement Then and Now

Immigration and Customs Enforcement (ICE) has adopted tougher standards in enforcing laws pertaining to the hiring of illegal immigrants. The following is a comparison of how ICE handled a particular case in March 2006 and how it might have been handled by the Immigration and Naturalization Service (INS), the government agency formerly assigned to enforcement:

ICE's approach in practice:

ICE executed search, arrest, and seizure warrants at three Kawasaki Restaurants—a small Japanese restaurant chain—[in Baltimore, MD] where we encountered fifteen undocumented workers living in deplorable conditions. Benefiting from their illegal workforce, the owners of the restaurants had created a lavish lifestyle for themselves. Fortunately, the three business owners were criminally arrested for money laundering and harboring of illegal aliens.

The owners have since pleaded guilty to these felony charges and agreed to forfeit approximately $1.1 million in assets.

How would this case have been handled differently prior to ICE's new approach? Historically, INS agents would have used administrative tools. They would have likely conducted an [employment verification] inspection at the Kawasaki Restaurants to determine whether the employer was in compliance.... Following the inspection, the issuance of a fine based on paperwork violations would have likely been the end result.

The maximum fine would have been approximately $20,000,—and in many cases, such a fine would be negotiated down even further, often down to half of the original penalty.

Immigrations and Customs Enforcement Web site, http://www.ice.gov/pi/news/factsheets/worksite_case_example.htm

sions to create a temporary-worker program, an enhanced visa system, tougher border controls and employer enforcement, and a path to citizenship for the country's 12 to 20 million illegal immigrants.

President George W. Bush, a supporter of immigration reform since he was Governor of Texas in the late 1990s, had urged Congress for years to create legislation reforming America's immigration system. "The agreement reached…is one that will help enforce our borders," the president said on May 17, 2007 after the Senate version of the bill was announced, "but equally importantly, it will treat people with respect."[59]

Written by Democrats who have traditionally been more concerned with immigrants' rights and Republicans who have often stressed the need for greater immigration enforcement, it was hoped that there was enough in the bill to please both parties and ensure passage. However, critics of the bill complained that it was so convoluted that it would actually please no one and either die without ever receiving a vote or pass and have no real effect on the immigration problem.

Ending Family Reunification Visas?

The bill called for changing the visa program, which stressed family ties, to a point system that favored skilled, educated workers with a level of English proficiency. In the past, visas were granted to individuals with relatives in the United States more readily than to lone workers, with the intent of keeping families together. However, familial unity is one of the biggest drivers of immigration, both legal and illegal, because people will more readily make the trip to the United States if there is someone there they trust who can help them find work and a place to live. By ending family reunification visas for the adult children and siblings of U.S. citizens, the government hoped to reduce the number of immigrants who come to the United States each year. In addition, by awarding points based on a person's job skills, education, and language ability, the new visas that are granted would go to workers whose abilities can be used by companies in need of employees who can positively contribute to the economy.

The temporary-worker program, which would allow 200,000 immigrants into the country for a period of up to two years, sought to address the need for cheap low-skilled workers called for by many American businesses. Temporary workers would not be allowed to bring family members, and they would be required to return to their native country after the two-year period with no opportunity to renew their status.

Z Visas

The most controversial element of the bill was the granting of Z Visas for illegal immigrants who came into the country before January 1, 2007. Z Visas would be renewable indefinitely provided that illegal immigrants paid a $5,000 fine, a $1,500 processing fee, and demonstrated a clean work and criminal background record. Republican Senator Kay Bailey Hutchison of Texas proposed extending the provision's "touchback" requirement to require all illegal immigrants to first return to their native country before applying for Z Visas. Some lawmakers considered this unworkable because illegal immigrants were not likely to come forward to announce their status if they knew they would have to leave the country with no sincere guarantee that they would be let back in legally. They would be just as likely to remain illegal and anonymous and take their chances as many have done for years.

Republican lawmakers equated the Z Visa provision with amnesty, recalling the 1986 IRCA law that granted amnesty to three million illegal immigrants and was viewed as a complete disaster by immigration control advocates. President Bush and Democratic Senator Edward Kennedy of Massachusetts, one of the bill's sponsors, said that the program was not amnesty because it compelled illegal immigrants to pay punitive fines. South Carolina Senator Jim DeMint disagreed. "This rewards people who broke the law with permanent legal status, and puts them ahead of millions of law-abiding immigrants waiting to come to America. I don't care how you try to spin it, this is amnesty."[60]

In order to draw support from Republicans like DeMint who did not agree with the Z Visa program, authors of the 2007 im-

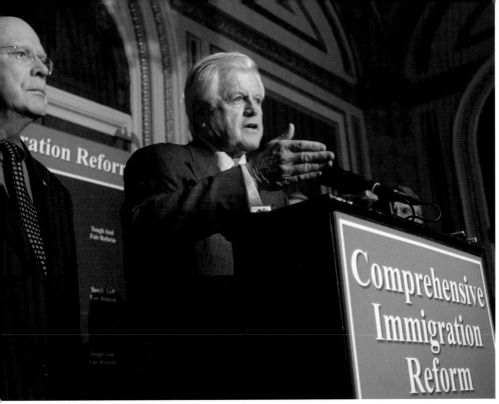

In May 2007 the U.S. Congress debated the pros and cons of a proposed immigration reform bill, but the bill failed to gain enough support for passage. Pictured here is Senator Edward Kennedy, right, of Massachusetts, one of the bill's sponsors.

migration package agreed to put all reform provisions on hold until after tougher border and employer enforcement procedures took effect. Before any other elements could be enacted, "the government must deploy 18,000 new Border Patrol agents and four unmanned aerial vehicles; build 200 miles of vehicle barriers, 370 miles of fencing, and 70 ground-based radar and camera towers; provide funds for the detention of 27,500 illegal immigrants a day; and complete new identification tools to help employers screen out illegal job applicants."[61]

Senate Democrats expressed concern that this was a stall tactic designed to keep what they believed were more meaningful reforms from taking place. Homeland Security Secretary Michael Chertoff maintained that this massive undertaking, which was already under way when the bill was written, could be completed in 18 months.

Senators voted on changes to the bill that would end the temporary worker program after five years and give federal authorities the power to investigate a person's immigration status. These proposed changes were defeated after fierce debate, and supporters of the bill had to defend it against accusations from conservative lawmakers that it was too lenient in its handling of illegal immigrants.

Many poor illegal immigrants feared just the opposite, and wondered how they would be able to raise the money to pay the fines and fees necessary to obtain a Z Visa. "Where would I get $5,000?" asked Daniel Carrillo Maldonado, an illegal immigrant in Phoenix, AZ. "In two years I don't get $5,000."[62] Others felt the fines are a small price to pay for gaining citizenship and all the benefits that came with it. "Compared with the better jobs you can get, it's nothing," said Karina Corona, an illegal worker in San Diego. "It's well worth it."[63]

THE PEOPLE CAN NOT WAIT

"The issue of immigration is too important for our elected officials to abandon. It cannot wait for several more years. Human beings are suffering and dying."

Bishop Gerald R. Barnes of San Bernardino, CA. Quoted in Robert Pear, "Broad Effort to Resurrect Immigration Bill," *New York Times*, June 16, 2007.

President Bush, who had trouble getting support from fellow Republican lawmakers to support the measure, suggested that enforcement provisions that were already in place were having a positive effect on the immigration problem. He pointed to the 30 percent drop in border arrests over a six-month period between October 2006 and April 2007, saying, "When you're apprehending few people, it means fewer are trying to come across. And fewer are trying to come across because we're deterring people from attempting illegal border crossings in the first place."[64]

The 2007 immigration reform bill failed to gain enough support for passage and was considered dead by the end of June. Although they vowed to make another attempt at passage, Bush, the bill's supporters in Congress, and the federal government as a whole faced a great deal of criticism from the public for not being able to successfully address the issue. Numerous state lawmakers also grew impatient at the lack of national leadership in immigration reform and took matters into their own hands.

The Role of the States in Reform

The federal government has set immigration policy in the United States since *Henderson v. Mayor of the City of New York,* an 1875 Supreme Court case which ruled that immigration policy fell under the federal government's constitutional authority to regulate interstate commerce. This arrangement worked relatively well until recently when the growing impact of illegal immigration created a strain on money for public services. Illegal immigrants benefited from services like education, health care, and living assistance for the poor which are often paid for and managed at local and state levels where governments are more closely involved with the people that they represent and are in tune with their needs. Since the arrival of illegal immigrants was mainly the result of the federal government's failure to maintain border security and immigration enforcement, local and state governments felt it was only fair for the federal government in Washington, DC, to provide assistance in meeting the shortfall created by the additional burden. In most cases, these requests were not honored.

"Federal authorities make decisions about the number and kind of immigrants to accept, but state, county and municipal authorities pick up the costs of absorption," notes Douglas S. Massey, professor of sociology at Princeton University. "Can we blame residents and officials in the cities for feeling put upon? They have no say about who comes to their municipalities, yet they must pay the bills." [65]

Without federal assistance or guidance, many states have acted on their own to deal with the issues of illegal immigration, assimilation, and the overall economic costs of immigration. Each state and city is different, and passes laws to meet their own needs. For instance, 30 U.S. states have enacted laws recognizing English as the official language of their state. Some of these laws go back many years, with Louisiana enacting its

Governor Richardson Declares a State of Emergency

In August 2005, New Mexico Governor Bill Richardson declared a state of emergency along the state's border with Mexico after widespread reports of problems related to illegal immigration. His action was symbolic of initiatives to curb illegal immigration taken by several state leaders who believed the federal government was not acting effectively to address the issue.

The following is a from a press release issued by Governor Richardson's office:

> "As Governor I have a responsibility to protect our citizens, property, and communities," said Governor Richardson. "Recent developments have convinced me this action is necessary—including violence directed at law enforcement, damage to property and livestock, increased evidence of drug smuggling, and an in-crease in the number of undocumented immigrants."

Governor Richardson's declaration makes $750,000 in state emergency funding immediately available to the affected counties. The Governor pledged an additional $1 million in assistance for the area. The funds will be used to support state and local law enforcement efforts, create and fund a field office for the New Mexico Office of Homeland Security to coordinate assistance to the area, and help build a fence to protect a livestock yard near Columbus, along a favorite path for illegal immigration where a number of livestock have been stolen and killed.

New Mexico Office of the Governor Web site, http://www.governor.state.nm.us/press/2005/august/081205_1.pdf

law in 1811, while others are in response to more recent events, like Idaho and Kansas, which enacted English recognition laws as recently as 2007.

Arizona enacted legislation that required business license applicants to prove legal presence in the United States. Pennsylvania debated a number of bills that would cut off non-emergency services to illegal immigrants and repeal the business licenses of companies that knowingly hired illegal workers. A similar bill to deny social services as well as in-state tuition overwhelmingly passed the Oklahoma House of Representatives, and became law in 2006 in Colorado and Georgia.

On the local level, some cities have gone in the opposite direction, granting a wide array of rights to illegal immigrants like social welfare programs and in some cases, even the right to vote. Additionally, these communities have denied local law enforcement the power to inquire about their immigration status. "Most of us know this town would have a heck of a time trying to run itself these days without the immigrants," said Hightstown, NJ, Mayor Robert Patten. "They're working at the grocery stores, the fast-food places, they're opening businesses and keeping this town alive and young."[66]

The laws passed by cities like Hightstown and San Francisco, CA, which has declared itself a place of sanctuary for illegal immigrants, run counter to federal law, but the civic leaders of these areas believe they have crafted a more realistic solution to the problem to suit the needs of their communities.

BREAKING THE LAW

"If they are going to be breaking laws and coming through the porous borders, they are going to suffer the consequences. I don't see where America is to blame."

Al Garza, executive director of the Minuteman Civil Defense Corps. Quoted in Brady McCombs, "Efforts to Cut Summer Deaths Along Border Aren't Working," *Tucson (Arizona) Daily Star,* June 24, 2007.

In cities and towns across America, citizens and their elected representatives are searching for the best possible solutions to reform immigration. Not everyone can agree as to what the best course of action will be that keeps the door open for millions of newcomers, insures the rights of citizens, and allows everyone to share in the American Dream. Whatever action is chosen must be done with care because future generations of Americans, both native- and foreign-born, will have to live with the decisions that are made in the coming months and years.

NOTES

Introduction: The Debate Over Immigration

1. CBS 2 News, Los Angeles, "Peaceful Protests End with Disturbance at March," May 2, 2007.

2. Daniel Gonzalez, "Marchers Re-Energized Amid Immigration Push," *Arizona Republic,* May 2, 2007.

Chapter One: The History of Immigration in America

3. Herbert S. Klein, *A Population History of the United States.* New York, Cambridge University Press, 2004, p. 83.

4. Francis Walker, "Restriction of Immigration," *The Atlantic Monthly,* June 1896.

Chapter Two: The New Face of Immigration

5. Tamar Jacoby, ed., *Reinventing the Melting Pot: The New Immigrants and What It Means to Be American.* New York: Basic Books, 2004, p. 17.

6. Federation for American Immigration Reform, "Immigration and Urban Sprawl," October 2002, http://www.fairus.org/site/PageServer?pagename=iic_immigrationissuecentersb1cc

7. Associated Press, "Census: Immigration Helps Big Metros Grow," April 5, 2007.

8. Associated Press, "Migration to U.S. Tops Death in Mexico," May 4, 2007.

9. Robert Justich and Betty Ng, CFA, "The Underground Labor Force Is Rising to the Surface," Bear Stearns Asset Management Inc., January 3, 2005, p. 3.

10. Michael Riley, "Criminal Crossing: Part 3: Border Sections in Arizona and Texas Are Hot Zones for Apprehensions, Where the Threat of Long Jail Terms Is Replacing 'the Inconvenience of Getting Caught,'" *Denver Post,* March 7, 2007.

11. Michael Martinez, "At 104 Degrees, the Forecast Is Death," *Chicago Tribune,* March 18, 2007.

12. Michael Martinez, "At 104 Degrees, the Forecast Is Death," *Chicago Tribune,* March 18, 2007.

13. Eunice Moscoso, "Study: Immigrants Don't Raise U.S. Crime Rate," *Arizona Daily Star,* February 27, 2007.

14. Patrick McGreevy, "Gang Crackdown Raises Touchy Issue," *Los Angeles Times,* March 10, 2007.

15. Patrick McGreevy and Richard Winton, "Feds to Bolster War on Gangs," *Los Angeles Times,* April 5, 2007.

Chapter Three: The Economics of Immigration

16. Daniel T. Griswold, "The Need for Comprehensive Immigration Reform: Serving Our National Economy," The Cato Institute, May 26, 2005.

17. Justich and Ng, "The Underground Labor Force Is Rising to the Surface," p. 2.

18. Griswold, "The Fiscal Impact of Immigration Reform: The Real Story," The Cato Institute, May 21, 2007.

19. Margaret Gibbons, "Program for Illegals Draws Fire," *Montgomery County Times Herald,* April 4, 2007.

20. Margaret Gibbons, "Program for Illegals Draws Fire," *Montgomery County Times Herald,* April 4, 2007.

21. Brandi Grissom, "Bill Would Raise Tuition for Undocumented Students," *El Paso Times,* April 2, 2007.

22. Brandi Grissom, "Bill Would Raise Tuition for Undocumented Students," *El Paso Times,* April 2, 2007.

23. Steven Camarota, "The High Cost of Cheap Labor," Center for Immigration Studies, August 2004, http://www.cis.org/articles/2004/fiscal.html.

24. Nina Bernstein, "Tax Returns Rise for Immigrants in U.S. Illegally," *New York Times,* April 16, 2007.

25. Nina Bernstein, "Tax Returns Rise for Immigrants in U.S. Illegally," *New York Times,* April 16, 2007.

26. Summer Harlow, "Filing Taxes Seen as Path to Citizenship," *Wilmington, DE, News Journal,* April 17, 2007.

27. Scott Miller, "Hispanic-Owned Business Booming in the United States," Washington File, April 12, 2006.

28. Thomas Sewell, "Myth Monopoly," *NationalReview.com,* May 22, 2007.

29. Griswold, "The Need for Comprehensive Immigration Reform: Serving Our National Economy," The Cato Institute, May 26, 2005.

30. Justich and Ng, "The Underground Labor Force Is Rising to the Surface," p. 2.

31. Steven Greenhouse, "Low Pay and Broken Promises Greet Guest Workers," *New York Times,* February 28, 2007.

32. Myung Oak Kim, Fernando Quintero, and Laura Frank, "Some Firms Play Loose with the Law," *Rocky Mountain News,* February 27, 2007.

33. Myung Oak Kim, Fernando Quintero, and Laura Frank, "Some Firms Play Loose with the Law," *Rocky Mountain News,* February 27, 2007.

34. Michael Riley, "U.S. Officials Want to Make the 2,000 Mile Southern Frontier Inhospitable to Crossers," *Denver Post,* March 5, 2007.

35. Jennifer Talhelm, "Immigration-Related Cases Clog Courts," *Associated Press,* April 27, 2007.

36. Michael Doyle, "Counties Receive Funds to Jail Criminal Aliens," *Fresno Bee,* February 23, 2007

Chapter Four: Assimilation and Identity

37. Peter D. Salins, *Reinventing the Melting Pot,* p. 102.

38. Samuel P. Huntington, *Who Are We? The Challenges to America's National Identity.* New York: Simon & Schuster, 2004, p. 12.

39. Huntington, *Who Are We?,* p. 142.

40. Luis R. Fraga and Gary M. Segura, "Culture Clash? Contesting Notions of American Identity and the Effects of Latin American Immigration," American Political Science Association Perspectives, June 2006, p. 281.

41. Peter Skerry, *Reinventing the Melting Pot,* p. 227.

42. Gregory Rodriguez, "Mexican Americans Are Building No Walls," *Los Angeles Times,* February 29, 2004.

43. Stephan Thernstrom, *Rediscovering the Melting Pot,* p. 52.

44. David Kennedy, "Can We Still Afford to Be a Nation of Immigrants?," *Atlantic Monthly,* November 1996, p. 67.

45. Kelley Beaucar Vlahos, "Becoming An American Likely to Get More Expensive Soon," Fox News, February 27, 2007.

46. Summer Harlow, "More Apply to Be Citizens," *Dallas Morning News,* March 19, 2007.

47. Mike Madden, "Backlash Fears Drive Efforts to Naturalize," *Arizona Republic,* February 23, 2007.

48. Jack Citrin, Amy Lerman, Michael Murakami, and Kathryn Pearson, "Testing Huntington: Is Hispanic Immigration a Threat to American Identity?", American Political Science Association Perspectives on Politics, March 2007, p. 35.

49. George J. Borjas, *Reinventing the Melting Pot,* p. 203.

Chapter Five: Calls for Reform

50. Teresa Watanabe and Anna Gorman, "Immigrant Advocates Gear Up," *Los Angeles Times,* March 17, 2007.

51. Teresa Watanabe and Anna Gorman, "Immigrant Advocates Gear Up," *Los Angeles Times,* March 17, 2007.

52. Sahra Susman, "Minuteman Group Wants to Shake Racist Image," *Ontario, California Daily Bulletin,* April 3, 2007.

53. Sahra Susman, "Minuteman Group Wants to Shake Racist Image," *Ontario, California Daily Bulletin,* April 3, 2007.

54. Nina Bernstein, "U.S. Raid on an Immigrant Household Deepens Anger and Mistrust," *New York Times,* April 10, 2007.

55. Nina Bernstein, "U.S. Raid on an Immigrant Household Deepens Anger and Mistrust," *New York Times,* April 10, 2007.

56. Elliot Spagat, "Immigration Raids Net Many Not on the Radar," *Associated Press,* April 6, 2007.

57. Elliot Spagat, "Immigration Raids Net Many Not on the Radar," *Associated Press,* April 6, 2007.

58. Alfonso Chardy, "New Tactic Hastens Deportations," *Miami Herald,* March 26, 2007.

59. Stephen Dinan, "Senate Immigration Deal Forged," *Washington Times,* May 18, 2007.

60. Stephen Dinan, "Senate Immigration Deal Forged," *Washington Times,* May 18, 2007.

61. Jonathan Weisman, "Deal on Immigration Reached," *Washington Post,* May 18, 2007.

62. Peter Prengaman, "Illegal Immigrants Question Senate Deal," *Associated Press,* May 19, 2007.

63. Peter Prengaman, "Illegal Immigrants Question Senate Deal," *Associated Press,* May 19, 2007.

64. Robert Pear, "Bush Ties Drop in Illegal Immigration to His Policies," *New York Times,* April 10, 2007.

65. Douglas S. Massey, *Reinventing the Melting Pot,* p. 118.

66. Anthony Faiola, "Looking the Other Way on Immigrants," *Washington Post,* April 10, 2007.

Chapter One: The History of Immigration in America

1. What factors limited immigration to America between 1789 and 1814?

2. How did public attitudes toward immigrants in the late 1800s affect immigration?

3. What direction did immigration in the U.S. take after Congress passed the Immigration and Nationality Act of 1965?

Chapter Two: The New Face of Immigration

1. According to the author, what two factors have historically influenced immigration to the United States?

2. How did the method Robert Justich and Betty Ng used to estimate the number of illegal immigrants differ from that used by the Census Bureau?

3. What are the pros and cons of the Los Angeles Police Department's Special Order 40?

Chapter Three: The Economics of Immigration

1. What did Texas State Representative Rick Noriega mean when he said, "Texas would be eating its seed corn" if it reversed the current tuition law?

2. How important are remittances to the Mexican economy?

3. Why are immigration laws more strictly enforced today versus a decade ago?

Chapter Four: Assimilation and Identity

1. How does Samuel Huntington's view of national identity differ from that of Fraga and Segura?

2. What facts imply that Hispanic immigrants are assimilating, and what facts imply they are not?

3. According to a study conducted in California, what are the advantages of bilingual education over English language immersion?

Chapter Five: Calls for Reform

1. What was the purpose of The Immigration Reform and Control Act of 1986 ?

2. In what ways would the U.S. visa program change under the Secure Borders, Economic Opportunity and Immigration Reform Act?

3. Why have states and cities passed immigration-related legislation despite an 1875 Supreme Court ruling that immigration policy is the responsibility of the federal government?

ORGANIZATIONS TO CONTACT

American Immigration Law Foundation
918 F Street, NW, 6th Floor
Washington, DC 20004
(202) 742-5600 • fax: (202) 742-5619
http://www.ailf.org

Dedicated to increasing public understanding of immigration law and policy and the value of immigration to American society, and to advancing fundamental fairness and due process under the law for immigrants.

The Brookings Institution
1775 Massachusetts Ave.
NW, Washington, DC 20036
(202) 797-6000 • fax: (202) 797-6004
http://www.brook.edu

The Brookings Institution is a private nonprofit organization devoted to independent research and innovative policy solutions

Department of Homeland Security
U.S. Department of Homeland Security
Washington, D.C. 20528
(202) 282-8000
http://www.dhs.gov

Cabinet-level department charged with protecting America from terrorist attacks.

Federation for American Immigration Reform
1666 Connecticut Avenue, NW, Suite 400
Washington, DC 20009
(202) 328-7004 • fax: (202) 387-3447
http://www.fairus.org

A national, nonprofit, public-interest, membership organization of concerned citizens who share a common belief that our nation's immigration policies must be reformed to serve the national interest.

Pew Research Center
1615 L Street, NW Suite 700
Washington, DC 20036
(202) 419-4300 • fax: (202) 419-4349
http://pewresearch.org

Nonpartisan organization that provides information on the issues, attitudes and trends shaping America and the world. It does so by conducting public opinion polling and social science research; by reporting news and analyzing news coverage; and by holding forums and briefings. It does not take positions on policy issues.

Books

Carl L. Bankston III and Danielle Antionette Hidalgo, editors, *Immigration in U.S. History*. Pasadena, CA: Salem Press, 2006. A comprehensive history of American immigration with anecdotes and personal stories of immigrants from all eras.

David M. Brownstone and Irene M. Frank, *Facts About American Immigration*. New York: H.W. Wilson Company, 2001. An encyclopedic volume of information about immigration spanning American history.

Peter Morton Coan, *Ellis Island Interviews: In Their Own Words*. New York: Checkmark Books, 1997. A collection of interviews with just some of the many people who came to American through Ellis Island.

Herbert S. Klein, *A Population History of the United States*. New York: Cambridge University Press, 2004. A statistical history of population growth in the United States with interesting facts about immigration and its affect on population.

James Loucky, Jeanne Armstrong, and Larry J. Estrada, editors, *Immigration in America Today*. Westport, CT: Greenwood Press, 2006. A comprehensive look at modern immigration in the United States and its possible future.

Monette Adeva Maglaya, *The Complete Success Guide for the Immigrant Life*. Glendale, CA: PDI Books, 2004. A handbook for immigrants in the U.S. that covers numerous topics, including historical facts, how to get a job, the value of money, popular leisure activities, and the dangers of too much television.

Web Sites

Center for Immigration Studies. (www.cis.org). Comprehensive Web site that features information, news articles, and

opinions favoring immigration control and reform in the U.S.

Contacto Magazine. (www.contactomagazine.com). English-language Web site devoted to detailing the Hispanic experience in the U.S., including news, business, politics, and entertainment.

Hispanic Business. (www.hispanicbusiness.com). A leading publication about Hispanic business in the United States. Includes news and information about the Hispanic marketplace.

National Immigration Forum. (www.immigrationforum.org). Comprehensive Web site with details on legislation, articles and opinions favoring less restriction in immigration.

The U.S. Census Bureau. (www.census.gov). Detailed statistical demographic and population information on the U.S. population dating back to the first census ever taken in 1790. Information about the foreign-born population and immigration history can also be found here.

U.S. Customs and Border Protection. (www.cbp.gov). Official Web site for the CBP, which handles the task of protecting America's borders. Learn about the CBP's job in great detail as well as what life is like for a Border Patrol agent.

U.S. House of Representatives Subcommittee on Immigration. (http://judiciary.house.gov/committeestructure. aspx?committee=4). Official Web site of the House subcommittee that handles immigration issues. This site offers up to date information on House legislative activity dealing with immigration reform.

U.S. Immigration and Customs Enforcement. (www.ice.gov). Official Web site for ICE, which enforces the nation's immigration laws as well as drug enforcement, smuggling, and other customs-related matters.

U.S. Senate Subcommittee on Immigration. (http://judiciary. senate.gov/subcommittees/110/immigration110.cfm). Official Web site of the Senate subcommittee that handles immigration issues. This site offers up to date information on Senate legislative activity dealing with immigration reform.

The U.S. Library of Congress: American Memory. (http://memory.loc.gov/ammem/index.html). The section on Immigration and American Expansion contains articles, narratives, and images about the history of immigration in America when many first person and historical accounts.

INDEX

Advocacy groups, 79–80
American Dream, 6, 95
American Protective Association (APA), 16
Americanization, 65
Appleby, Kevin, 71–72
Applications for citizenship, 71–72
Apprehension, of illegal immigrants, 34–38
Arizona, 9, 24, 72, 81, 94
Army National Guard, 59–60
Asian immigrants, 11, 27, 42, 65
Assimilation issues, 62–76
   acquiring English languages skills,
     73–75
American identity evolution, 64–67
   bilingual vs. English-only immersion,
     75–76
   citizenship applications, 71–72
   of Hispanics, 67–70
   for Latin American immigrants, 64
Atlantic Monthly (Walker), 19–20
Australia, 17

Baby Boomers, 51
Bear Stearns Asset Management, Inc. immigrant report, 33–34, 42–43
Bilingual vs. English-only immersion,
   75–76
Border, U.S.-Mexico, 24, 33, 69
Border Patrol agents, 24, 36, 59, 60, 91
   deployment of Army National Guard,
     58–59
   economics of securing, 43, 58–61
   informing immigrants of dangers, 37
   injuries crossing, 46
   Minuteman Civil Defense Corps, 81
   need for increased presence, 36, 77, 79
   Secure Border Initiative, 59
   state of emergency declaration, 94
Bracero Program, 23
Bush, George W.,89, 90, 92

California, 70
   Border Patrol success, 24
   Chinese railroad workers, 21
   Coalition for Immigration Reform, 37

English language immersion programs,
   76
   Gold Rush, 17, 21
   major migration to, 30, 70
   reimbursement for law enforcement, 61
Camarota, Steven, 48
Catholic immigrants, 18, 19, 64
Cato Institute (Washington, D.C.), 42
Census Bureau (U.S.), 12, 26–27, 32–34
Center for Human Rights and Constitutional
   Law, 80
Center for Immigration Studies, 48
Chertoff, Michael, 91
Chicago demonstrations, 7, 9
China, 17, 21
Chinese Exclusion Act (1882), 21
Chinese immigrants, 21
Citizenship, 9–10, 32, 46, 66, 71–72
Citizenship and Immigration Services (CIS)
   Bureau, 71
Civic/labor organizations, 80
Civil War, 17, 64
Clark, Randy, 59
Columbia University, 82–83
Conference of Catholic Bishops, 71–72
Construction companies, 55–56
Copper Queen Hospital free care, 45–46
Cornell University Cooperative Extension of
   Hispanic dairy workers, 30
"The Cost of Illegal Immigration to New
   Yorkers" report, 63
Council of the Americas, 52
Current Population Survey, 33–34
Customs and Border Patrol (CBP), 58

Dalmia, Shikha, 78
Declaration of Independence (U.S.), 64
DeMint, Jim, 90–91
Democratic lawmakers, 91
Demonstrations (protests) by immigrants,
   6, 7–9
Department of Homeland Security (DHS),
   33–34, 58, 59, 91, 94
Department of Labor, Wage and Hour
   (U.S.), 57
Deportation

1954, of Mexican immigrants, 23–24
2006/2007 statistics, 10
of illegal immigrants, 34–38, 85–87
Dillingham, William, 21–22

Economics of immigration, 42–61
    costs of border patrol, 58–61
    educational access, 47–48
    growth of economic burden, 44–45
    healthcare access, 45–47
    Hispanic market, 51–52
    low-skilled laborers, 52–58
    New York State, 63
    taxation issues, 48–51
Educational access, 47–48, 75–76
Ellis Island reception center (New York),
    18, 20, 21
Emergency Quota Act (1921), 22
Enforcement, of immigration, 83
Ethnic/language diversity, countries with, 66
European immigration
    Southern/Eastern, 17–20, 65
    Western Europe, 13–17, 65
Everson, Mark W., 49
Expectations of immigrants, 62–63
Exploitation of immigrants, 57

Factfinder for the Nation (Census Bureau),
    12
FAIR (Federation for American Immigration
    Reform), 30–31, 63
Family reunification visas, 89–90
Farnsworth, Eric, 52
Federal attempts at immigration reform,
    87–89
Federation for American Immigration
    Reform (FAIR), 30–31, 63
Florida, 30, 70
Food stamps, lack of access, 44–45
Fraga, Luis R., 66, 67
France, 14, 66
French Revolution (1789), 13

German-Americans, 68–69
Germany, 14, 17
Gold Rush (California), 17, 21
Great Britain, 14, 17
Great Depression, 22
Green cards (Permanent Resident Cards), 71
Griswold, Daniel T., 42, 44
Gross domestic product (GDP)
    of Mexico, 29
    of U.S., 26
Guatemalan immigrants, 30

Hahamovitch, Cindy, 55
Harvard University, 68
Healthcare access, 45–47
Henderson v. Mayor of the City of New
    York (1875), 93
Heritage Foundation, 44
Hindus, 66
Hispanic immigrants
    assimilation issues, 67–70
    geographic concentrations, 70
Hispanic/Latino market profile, 51
Hispanic Television Index, 29
    market growth in U.S., 51–52
    support of native country family, 51
Honduran immigrants, 30
Housing conditions for immigrants, 19
Huntington, Samuel, 43, 64, 68
Hutchison, Kay Bailey, 90

ICRA (Immigration Reform and Control
    Act), 77
Illegal immigrants
    Census counting, 32–34
    jailing/deportation of, 34–38
    lack of social program access, 44–45
    low-skilled jobs, 7, 10, 42, 52–58
    penalties for hiring, 55, 57
    prenatal care programs, 46
    taxation issues, 42, 48–49, 78
Immigrants
    blocking of, 20–22
    expectations of, 62–63
    exploitation of, 57
    illegal immigrants, 10
    poverty among, 38–41
    religions of, 18, 19, 64
    See also Illegal immigrants; specific
        nationalities (e.g., Irish immigrants,
        Latin American immigrants, etc.)
Immigration, economics of, 42–61
    costs of border patrol, 58–61
    educational access, 47–48
    growth of economic burden, 44–45
    healthcare access, 45–47
    Hispanic market, 51–52
    low-skilled laborers, 52–58
    taxation issues, 48–51
Immigration and Custom Enforcement (ICE)
    know your rights presentations, 86
    raids performed by, 34–35, 57, 83–85
    standards for law enforcement, 88
Immigration and Nationality Act (1965),
    24–25
Immigration Commission (U.S.), 21

Immigration enforcement, 83
Immigration history, in U.S., 11–25
  blocking of immigrants, 20–22
Immigration and Nationality Act (1965),
  24–25
  southern/eastern Europe immigration,
    17–20
  twentieth century, 22–24
  western European immigration, 13–17
Immigration reform, federal attempts at,
  87–89. *See also* Reform of immigration.
Immigration Reform and Control Act
  (ICRA), 77
Immigration Reform Unity Blueprint, 80–81
India, 66
Internal Revenue Service (IRS), 49
Irish immigrants, 15, 18, 19, 64, 82
Italy, 17

Jackson, Jim, 48
Jacoby, Tamara, 26
Jailing, of illegal immigrants, 34–38
Jewish immigrants, 19, 64, 82
Jobs, low-skilled, 7, 10, 42, 52–58
Justich, Robert, 33–34, 42

Kennedy, Edward, 90, 91
Klein, Herbert S., 16
Ku Klux Klan (KKK), 16, 82

Labor laws, 42
Latin American immigrants, 25, 27, 28–38
  apprehension of, 34–38
  assimilation challenges, 64
  Census counting of, 32–34
  impact on American cities, 30–32
  poverty/crime rates, 38–41
  Spanish language television, 29
Latinvox company (for Hispanic market), 52
Legalization path, 80
Legislation
  Emergency Quota Act (1921), 22
  Immigration and Nationality Act (1965),
    24–25
  Immigration Reform and Control Act,
    77
  McCarren-Walter Immigration Act
    (1952), 23
  National Origins Act (1924), 22
  Secure Border Initiative, 59
  Secure Borders Economic Opportunity
    and Immigration Reform Act, 88
  War Brides Act (1945/46), 23
Library of Congress, 16

Literacy tests, 21
Los Angeles demonstrations, 7

Magazine Publishers of America, 51
Massey, Douglas S., 93
Mayor of the City of New York, Henderson
  v. (1875), 93
McCarren-Walter Immigration Act (1952),
  23
Medicare, lack of access, 44–45
Mexican immigrants
  2000 statistics, 31–32
  Bracero Program, 23
Mexican War, 17
Mexico-U.S. border, 24, 33, 69
  deployment of Army National Guard,
    58–59
  economics of securing, 43, 58–61
  informing immigrants of dangers, 37
  injuries crossing, 46
  Minuteman Civil Defense Corps, 81–83
  need for increased presence, 36, 77, 79
  Secure Border Initiative, 59
  state of emergency declaration, 94
Minuteman Civil Defense Corps, 81–83
Multiculturalism, 65–66
Muslims, 66

Napoleonic Wars, 13
National Council of La Raza (NCLR), 45
National Origins Act (1924), 22
National Research Council, 78
Naturalization. *See* Citizenship
NCLR (National Council of La Raza), 45
New America Foundation, 68
New York City, Ellis Island reception cen-
  ter, 18, 20, 21
New York State, cost of illegal immigra-
  tion, 63
Ng, Betty, 33–34, 42
Noriega, Rick, 48
NumbersUSA immigration control group,
  81–83

Office of Management and Budget (White
  House), 61
Operation Streamline, 60
Order of the Star-Spangled Banner, 18–19
Order of United Americans, 18–19

Pearson, Kathryn, 73, 75
Penalties, for hiring illegal immigrants, 55,
  57–58
Permanent Resident Cards (green cards), 71
Pew Research Center survey, 70

Poland, 17
A Population History of the United States
    (Klein), 16
Poverty, among immigrants, 38–41
Prenatal care programs, 46
Princeton University, 93
Protestant immigrants, 18

Racism, 19
Raids, 57
    call for end, 9
    performed by ICE, 34–35, 57, 83–85
Railroad construction, 16
Reason Foundation think tank, 78
Reform of immigration
    attempts at federal level, 87–89
    Federation for American Immigration
        Reform, 30–31, 63
    Immigration Reform and Control Act,
        77
    role of states, 93–95
    Secure Borders Economic Opportunity
        and Immigration Reform Act, 88
    Unity Blueprint for Immigration
        Reform, 80–81
*Reinventing the Melting Pot: The New
    Immigrants and What it Means to be an
    American* (ed. Jacoby), 26, 63
Religions of immigrants, 18, 19, 64
Republican lawmakers, 77
Richardson, Bill, 94
Rodriguez, Gregory, 68
Roynman, Joseph, 46
Russia, 17

Salins, Peter D., 63
Schey, Peter, 80
Secure Border Initiative (SBInet), 59–60
Secure Borders Economic Opportunity and
    Immigration Reform Act, 88
Segura, Gary M., 66, 67
Skerry, Peter, 66–67
Slavery, 64
Social welfare needs, 43
South America, 17
Southern Europe immigration, 17–20
Spain, 66
Spanish language television, 29
Spanish speaking immigrants, 73, 75
Stanford University, 66
States' role in immigration reform, 93–95
Supreme Court decisions
    Chinese Exclusion Act, 21
    Henderson v. Mayor of the City of New
        York, 93

Passenger Case, 20

Taxation issues, 42, 48–51, 78
Temporary visas, 6
Terrorism, 58
Texas, 24, 29, 30, 36, 47, 48, 70, 89
Thernstrom, Stephan, 68–69
Trade Policy Studies (Cato Institute), 42
Tuberculosis, 21
Twentieth century immigration, 22–24

Unemployment benefits, lack of access,
    44–45
United States
    Army National Guard, 59–60
    Bureau of Citizenship and Immigration
        Services, 71
    Census Bureau, 12, 26–27, 32–34
    Civil War, 17, 64
    Declaration of Independence, 64
    Department of Homeland Security,
        33–34, 58, 59, 91, 94
    Department of Labor, Wage and Hour,
        57
    economic differences with Mexico,
        69–70
    Hispanic market growth, 51–52
    history of immigration, 11–25
    Immigration Commission, 21
    impact of Latin American immigration,
        30–32
    Office of Management and Budget, 61
Unity Blueprint for Immigration Reform,
    80–81
University of California, Berkeley, 73
University of Minnesota, 73
University of Washington, 66
Urban Institute, 33–34

Visas
    family reunification visas, 89–90
    temporary visas, 6
    Z visas, 90–93

Walker, Francis, 19
War Brides Act (1945/1946), 23
Washington, D.C. demonstrations, 9
Western European immigration, 13–17
White House, Office of Management and
    Budget, 61
*Who Are We? The Challenge to America's
    National Security* (Huntington), 43, 64
World Trade Center, 58
World War II, Bracero Program, 23

PICTURE CREDITS

Cover: © Martyn Goddard/
  Corbis
AP Images, 7, 8, 35, 47, 50, 56,
  59, 65, 67, 71, 74, 79, 81, 84,
  87, 91
Cengage Learning, Gale, 13, 14,
  28
Alex Wong/Getty Images, 15
© North Wind Picture Archives,
  18
The Library of Congress, 20
© Leonard Nadel/National

Museum of American History/
  Handout/Reuters/Corbis, 23
Lyndon Baines Johnson Library,
  24
Sarah Caron/Getty Images, 33,
  36
Robert Nickelserg/Getty Images,
  39
Suzy Allman/Getty Images, 41
Justin Sullivan/Getty Images, 53
© Andrew Holbrooke/Corbis, 60
Joe Raedle/Getty Images, 73

ABOUT THE AUTHOR

This is Richard Brownell's fourth title for Lucent Books. His other books include *The Fall of the Confederacy* and *The End of Slavery*, and *America's Failure in Vietnam*, which are part of Lucent's History's Great Defeats series, and *The Oklahoma City Bombing*, which is part of Lucent's Crime Scene Investigation Series. He has written two stage plays that have received numerous productions around the country, and also writes political commentary for various periodicals and Internet sites. He holds a Bachelor of Fine Arts degree from New York University, where he was also recognized for Senior Achievement in Screenwriting. Richard lives in New York City.